WATER RESOURCES INFORMATION AND ISSUES OVERVIEW REPORT

BENT'S OLD FORT NATIONAL HISTORIC SITE

Natural Resource Report NPS/NRPC/WRD/NRR—2010/258

David L. Vana-Miller
Water Resources Division
Natural Resource Program Center
P.O. Box 25287
Denver, CO 80225

Courtney Moore
Bent's Old Fort National Historic Site
35110 Highway 194 East
La Junta, CO 81050

Jeff Hughes
Water Resources Division
Natural Resource Program Center
1201 Oak Ridge Dr., Suite 250
Fort Collins, CO 80525

Kevin F. Noon
Water Resources Division
Natural Resource Program Center
P.O. Box 25287
Denver, CO 80225

October 2010

U.S. Department of the Interior
National Park Service
Natural Resource Program Center
Fort Collins, Colorado

The National Park Service, Natural Resource Program Center publishes a range of reports that address natural resource topics of interest and applicability to a broad audience in the National Park Service and others in natural resource management, including scientists, conservation and environmental constituencies, and the public.

The Natural Resource Report Series is used to disseminate high-priority, current natural resource management information with managerial application. The series targets a general, diverse audience, and many contain NPS policy considerations or address sensitive issues of management applicability.

All manuscripts in the series receive the appropriate level of peer review to ensure that the information is scientifically credible, technically accurate, appropriately written for the intended audience, and designed and published in a professional manner. This report received informal peer review by subject-matter experts who were not directly involved in the collection, analysis, or reporting of the data.

Views, statements, findings, conclusions, recommendations, and data in this report do not necessarily reflect views and policies of the National Park Service, U.S. Department of the Interior. Mention of trade names or commercial products does not constitute endorsement or recommendation for use by the U.S. Government.

This report is available from the Natural Resource Publications Management website (http://www.nature.nps.gov/publications/NRPM).

Please cite this publication as:

Vana-Miller, D., C. Moore, J. Hughes and K. Noon. 2010. Water resources information and issues overview report: Bent's Old Fort National Historic Site. Natural Resource Report NPS/NRPC/WRD/NRR—2010/258. National Park Service, Fort Collins, Colorado.

NPS 417/105853, October 2010

Contents

Figures

Tables

Executive Summary

This Water Resources Information and Issues Overview Report is one of several planning products offered by the National Park Service Water Resources Division that assists national park units with achieving or maintaining water resource integrity.

Bent's Old Fort National Historic Site (NHS) is a 799.8-acre national park unit in Otero County of southeastern Colorado, approximately 7.5 miles northeast of the town of La Junta. The park was authorized in 1960 for the purpose of establishing a national historic site at the location of Bent's Old Fort on the Santa Fe Trail. The NHS commemorates the Bent-St. Vrain Trading Empire, which radiated from Bent's Old Fort into what are now Texas, New Mexico, Kansas, Nebraska, Arizona, Utah, Wyoming and Missouri. Bent's Old Fort was an important point of commercial, social, military, and cultural contact between Anglo-American, Native Tribes, Hispanic, and various minority cultures on the border of the U. S. Territory. The original adobe fort was constructed in 1833 on the edge of a low, floodplain terrace, approximately 300 yards from the Arkansas River. This location served the strategic purpose of furthering trade along the Santa Fe Trail.

This *Water Resources Information and Issues Overview Report* was developed at the request of the NHS. It represents an important collation and summarization of water resource information; an identification of applicable federal, state and local legislation and policy that affect the management water resources; an assessment of current water resource status; and, an identification and analysis of water resource issues that the NHS is currently facing, and recommends future management actions or directions to address those issues.

The report is organized into four major sections. The first, *Introduction*, describes the NHS, outlines the laws, regulations, and policies relevant to water resource management at the NHS, and describes the varying roles of federal, state, regional, and local agencies in water resources management along the Arkansas River.

The second section, *Description of Resources*, describes the NHS and its surrounding area in terms of climate, physiography, geology/soils, land use, surface and ground water hydrology and quality, wetlands and riparian areas, and aquatic biological resources. It also describes the geomorphology of the Arkansas River.

The third section, *Water Resource Issues and Recommendations*, describes the water resource issues identified by NHS staff during an internal scoping process. In addition, this section provides recommendations for future action or direction that NHS management may consider. Water resource issues and recommendations are as follows:

- Water Rights and Ground Water Wells

    Water rights information should be updated to fill in missing information as to the history and present status of NHS water rights for both the park files and NPS Water Rights Branch dockets. In order to accomplish this task, files from the Colorado Division of

Water Resources, Fort Lyon Canal Company, and the Colorado Water Court should be reviewed and copies made of missing information for each well and ditch right. Submitting a Technical Assistance request to the NPS, Water Resources Division is an option if the NHS does not have the staff or expertise in this matter. Also, an analysis should be made by the NHS as to its current and future water needs to determine if existing NHS water rights are adequate. If certain wells and/or water rights are no longer needed, an effort to properly abandon the well(s) and right(s) should be undertaken. Since more irrigation use is planned for other areas of the NHS, an effort should be made to see if the NHS shares in the Fort Lyons Canal Company could be exchanged for the right to divert tributary ground water from the Arkansas River basin.

- Water Quality and Quantity of the Arkansas River

An effort by the NPS in 1998 provided a basic retrospective analysis of water quality conditions at those monitoring stations with records in STORET, the national water quality database. In our estimation that analysis was and is of limited value to the NHS, simply because the closest upstream station with an adequate period of record is in La Junta, 8 miles west of the NHS. The closest downstream station is on the Arkansas River at Hadley, CO (USGS #07123300 and BEOL 7), two miles downstream. However, that station has been inactive since the 1980's and has a very limited period of record that did not measure discharge. The La Junta station (USGS #07123000) has an adequate period of record (in some cases > 50 years and current) for most of the five core water quality vital signs. Additionally, other important constituents (e.g. calcium, sulfate, selenium) also have adequate periods of record. Most importantly, discharge is measured at this station. Because there are no permanent water inputs to the Arkansas River between La Junta and the NHS, the analysis of water quality data from the La Junta station would provide useful information. We recommend that the NHS submit a technical assistance request to the NPS Water Resources Division for a status and trends analysis of water quality and discharge information for the La Junta station.

We recommend two options for the establishment of routine water quality monitoring of the Arkansas River at the NHS. First, the Southern Plains Inventory and Monitoring Network (SOPN) could establish a core vital signs monitoring site just downstream of the west boundary of the NHS; a quarterly sampling frequency would be the minimum. These water quality data could be correlated with the discharge data of the La Junta station. Additionally, the network could data mine the La Junta site for other important constituents. Second, the network or NHS could totally rely on the mining of discharge and water quality data from the La Junta station.

Routine monitoring of biological condition is an important tool in understanding overall water resource condition. Because the sampling, identification, and analysis of the aquatic macroinvertebrate community require specialized expertise, we do not recommend this as something to be accomplished by the NHS. The SOPN would be the NPS entity better suited for the lead in such an assessment; however, understanding aquatic biological condition is not a SOPN vital sign, and may be of low priority.

Colorado's Ecological Monitoring and Assessment Program (EMAP) within the Colorado Department of Public Health and the Environment developed bioassessment tools for use in monitoring and assessing streams statewide. We recommend that the NHS contact the Colorado Department of Public Health and the Environment and propose that the State sample the Arkansas River macroinvertebrate community within the boundaries of the NHS as an additional stressed site. This would be a limited assessment to assist the State with refining its macroinvertebrate assessment tool of the Colorado plains. For the long-term, perhaps the NHS and State could develop a Memorandum of Agreement for the State to monitor the macroinvertebrate community of the Arkansas River at the NHS on a recurring basis as part of a statewide assessment of stream biological condition.

- High Water Table and Impacts to Bent's Old Fort

Given that ground water quantity is a vital sign of the SOPN, we agree with the recommendations by outlined by a Texas State University study in 2007 for the SOPN, namely:

- Historic and future ground water elevation data should be consolidated within an electronic database and coordinated with the operation of an appropriate national or state-related database, and
- Given the connection between periodically high water tables and flooding of the Fort, the NHS should renovate at least a select few of the PVC-lined, hand augured and well-point driven piezometers installed in 2002 for a previous study and renew efforts to monitor ground water elevations.

With regard to the first recommendation, we suggest that the NHS submit a technical assistance request to the NPS Water Resources Division for assistance with the database and any integration with national/state databases.

With regard to the second recommendation, we suggest the renovation of five wells that represent either a close association with the Fort and lack of correlation with river stage or a strong correlation with river stage due to floodplain locations. Water table elevations in these wells should be monitored monthly and linked with monthly-monitored levels at two Arkansas River staff gages and other appropriate benchmarks. This will link river stage levels with hydraulic head.

For the present, we do not agree with a 2002 recommendation that a more detailed term study of different water sources and aquifer properties is needed to parse out of the relative effects of river, canal and excess irrigation on water table levels and basement flooding at the Fort. Such knowledge, while of heuristic value, would do little in terms of improving knowledge and mitigating the flooding problem. That basement flooding of the Fort is caused by a combination of high river stage and canal seepage/excess irrigation is of high scientific probability based on a previous study. Therefore, barring the improbable -- moving the location of the Fort, the NHS should center its energy on mitigation and remediation of the Fort basement, although the available methods are limited. In addition, the NHS should work with such local entities as the

Southeast Colorado Resource Conservation and Development Council to understand and mitigate the amount of excess irrigation and canal leakage flowing towards the NHS.

- Wetland and Riparian Protection

We concur with a previous recommendation to periodically monitor the aquatic plants and animals and recommend a recurrence interval of every five years. Additionally, we recommend monitoring for a suite of water quality parameters in the NHS wetlands and would specifically include pH, temperature, dissolved oxygen, specific conductance, nitrogen (dissolved ammonia, total ammonia + organic, dissolved nitrate and nitrite, and dissolved nitrite), and phosphorus (dissolved and ortho-phosphorus dissolved). Sampling locations should be fixed; in the case of the Arch and Casebolt wetlands, sampling should occur at the previous well monitoring sites for those wetlands. Sampling frequency, initially, should be quarterly, and depending upon the analysis of data for a three to five year timeframe, sampling could occur annually (summer). Additionally, we recommend the establishment of a monitoring station on the Arch Wetland that is down gradient from the septic system at the Fort – this site should be monitored at least quarterly for nitrogen and phosphorus constituents.

We agree with a previous recommendation to renovate the monitoring wells established in 2002 in the Arch and Casebolt wetlands. Ground water elevations should be recorded on a monthly basis and linked with levels at Arkansas River staff gages, other ground water monitoring wells, and other appropriate benchmarks so that that all sites can be associated with hydraulic head and stream stage.

We recommend that the artificial wetlands (Day Pond, Day Wetland, and stock tank wetlands) be managed for their wetland functions, which include floodwater storage/attenuation, ground water recharge, amphibian breeding habitat, and other wildlife habitat.

It is recommended that the NHS submit a technical assistance request to the NPS Water Resources Division for an assessment of the riparian conditions along the Arkansas River using *The Process for Assessing Proper Functioning Condition*. We recommend that the recurrence interval for additional assessments be every five years.

Additionally, the NHS should establish GPS-based photograph points on the banks of the Arkansas River. Photographic monitoring is a simple and inexpensive method to assess changes in stream geomorphology, the riparian zone, and other physical habitat features that may be associated with site and watershed conditions. A series of photographs would also allow detection of slow, progressive changes in physical habitat features that otherwise might go undetected until the accumulation of impacts is noticeable.

- Flooding and Stormwater Drainage

Storm drainage around the NHS employee entrance road to the maintenance yard and administration building is a problem during most heavy rain events. A drainage ditch runs along the west side of the road. One possible solution to the drainage problem is to design an outfall at the south end of the ditch. A ditch and/or culvert extension should be placed to allow positive drainage from the south end of the existing ditch to an area that is lower in elevation. It appears from field observations that one option would be to run a culvert to the southeast under the entry road that would day light at a lower elevation in the open field. Since the area seems relatively flat, the culvert may have to be quite long in order to meet grade at a lower elevation in the field. The low areas in the field have water lines and sewer pump station pipes that may or may not allow deposition of sheet flow from the ditch. Another option is to continue the ditch and culverts to the south along the entry road. However, this would end up contributing to the existing drainage system that is further south, which serves the parking lot for the visitor center, and the additional flow may overload that system. The following tasks need to be completed in order to identify, select, and implement the best solution:

- o Complete a detailed topographic survey (no more than one-foot contour elevations) of the entire drainage ditch including culvert inverts, and the survey should also include the area at least 100 feet on either side of the existing ditch, the area around the southern end of the ditch including the road south to the visitor center parking lot, and the open field area (for several hundred feet east of the entry road).
- o Analyze the topography to determine the best solution. Consider the length of culvert necessary depending on the amount of drop in elevation needed to move the water, clogging and maintenance problems, potential erosion problems, and impacts to other infrastructure. Also consider other options including detention basin(s).
- o Replace all of the culverts in, and dredge, the existing ditch. Since the culvert is acting like a detention basin, the sediment laden water collects in the ditch, slows down, and deposits sediment such that the culverts are half-buried and the ditch is filling with silt.

- Sewage Treatment and Septic Systems

We recommend the monitoring of nitrogen and phosphorus as part of a monitoring program for the Arch Wetland.

- Hazardous Waste Management and Spill Contingency Planning

The NHS should strongly consider developing an Oil Spill Prevention and Response Plan. Such a plan would present site-specific information on those locations in the NHS that have the potential to experience such environmental change. In addition, general structural and operational recommendations would be outlined to prevent spills associated with all on-site activities involving the storage and/or use of petroleum products or other hazardous materials. A notification sequence, including emergency contacts, would be provided if a spill occurs. The Plan would be intended for use by all personnel responsible for storage, handling, and removal of hazardous substances at the NHS.

The fourth and final section, *Water Resources of Bent's Old Fort National Historic Site and Climate Change*, briefly describes the possible future water resource conditions under projected climate scenarios.

Acknowledgments

We would like to express our sincere appreciation to Alexa Roberts and Fran Pannebaker, Superintendent and Chief of Natural Resources for Bent's Old Fort National Historic Site, respectively, for their support during the development of this document and their perseverance in dealing with the numerous delays in publication of this report. We also thank the staff of the Maintenance Division for providing information on water-based infrastructure at the NHS. We thank the following individuals who reviewed the report and provided helpful comments: Fran Pannebaker; Robert Bennetts; John Reber; Mark Flora; Mike Martin; and Don Weeks.

Introduction

Park Location and Description

Bent's Old Fort National Historic Site (NHS) is a 799.8-acre national park unit in Otero County of southeastern Colorado, approximately 7.5 miles northeast of the town of La Junta (Figure 1). It is bordered on the north by State Highway 194 and on the south by U.S. Highway 50. Approximately 2.28 river miles of the Arkansas River flow within the boundary of the NHS.

In 1960, PL 86-487 authorized the park unit for the purpose of establishing a national historic site at the location of Bent's Old Fort on the Santa Fe Trail. The original site contained 178 acres; approximately 622 acres were added to the NHS by PL 95-625 in 1978. The Santa Fe Trail was designated a National Historic Trail by PL 100-35 in 1987.

The historic site commemorates the Bent-St. Vrain Trading Empire, which radiated from Bent's Old Fort into what are now Texas, New Mexico, Kansas, Nebraska, Arizona, Utah, Wyoming and Missouri. Bent's Old Fort was an important point of commercial, social, military, and cultural contact between Anglo-American, Native Tribes, Hispanic, and various minority cultures on the border of the U. S. Territory (NPS 1994).

The original adobe fort was constructed in 1833 on the edge of a low floodplain, terrace, approximately 300 yards from the Arkansas River. It served as a trade center on the Santa Fe Trail. For much of the original fort's history it was the only major permanent white settlement on the Trail. In addition to supplying goods to the pioneers and the military, the fort became a staging area for the U.S. Army during the Mexican War in 1846. The fort was abandoned in 1849.

Gardner (2004) described the Arkansas River as a directional beacon and landmark for overland travelers. The Arkansas River was, at the time of the original fort, the border between the U.S. and New Mexico. The fort's location along the Arkansas River was a strategic position to further the main purpose of the Fort -- trade along the Santa Fe Trail. Vital natural resources were provided by the Arkansas River.

According to historical accounts, the Arkansas River near the fort was a large, meandering river with semi-turbid water, a gravel bottom, a rapid current of 4-6 miles/hr, and sparsely populated with cottonwoods and diverse types of life (Swenson 1970). The river was shallow enough in places to be forded, accessing trade routes to the south -- an important crossing could possibly have been located just east of the fort.

Droughts spurred the change from the dryland farming of the 1880's to the development of diversion and irrigation programs using water from today's Arkansas River. This new recharge to the river, in effect, raised the water table above the river bed in late summer and changed the hydrologic character of the river from intermittent to perennial (Nadler and Schumm 1981). These irrigation programs and associated water rights have a long history of litigation between farmers, canal companies, and states all contending for limited water rights. Some of this conflict was mitigated by the construction of John Martin and Pueblo dams, downstream and upstream of the NHS, respectively, which serve as storage for winter runoff and flood waters,

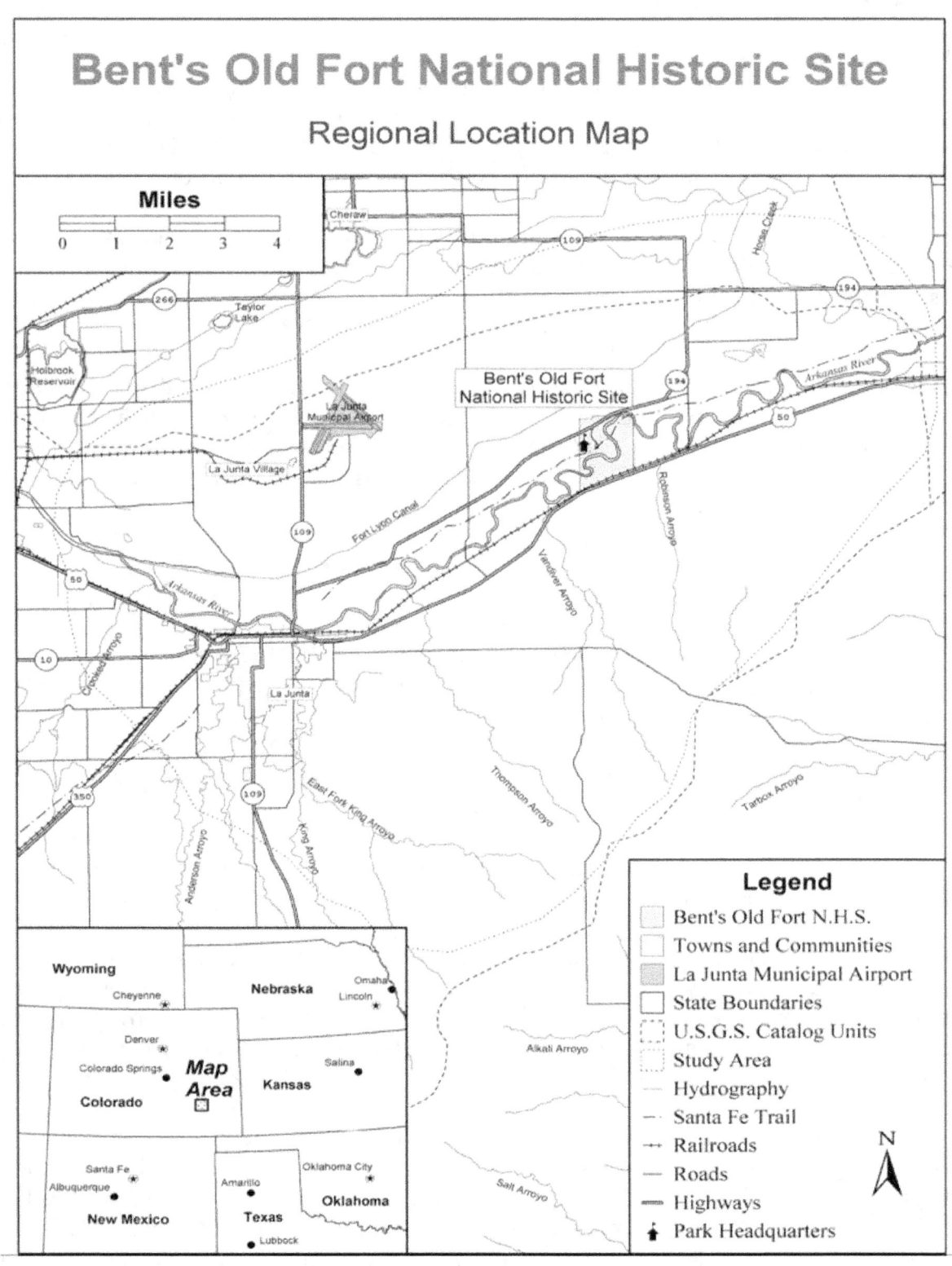

Figure 1. Map of Bent's Old Fort NHS and surrounding area (from NPS 1998).

and regulate the flow of the river. Drought and water rights continue to be challenges. Presently, there is pressure to divert water to growing urban areas along the Front Range.

Importance of Planning to Water Resources Management

Water is a particularly important and sensitive ecosystem component, and it plays a central role in the social, economic, environmental, and political mosaic of our national park units. Its physical availability and quality are critical determinants of a park's overall natural resource condition. Because of the important role of water in maintaining resource condition, it is the policy of the NPS to maintain, rehabilitate, and perpetuate the inherent natural integrity of water resources and water-dependent environments occurring within national park system units.

Proper management of water resources within the NPS is becoming more complex and challenging as threats to these resources, both internal and external to park boundaries, increase. Scientists and managers are increasingly called upon to respond to disruptions of water resources that threaten the quality of human life and environmental sustainability. Planning is an essential first step in addressing these threats and disruptions. The Planning Program of the Water Resources Division (WRD) of the NPS has assisted in the development of park-wide management strategies and ensured that park managers and policy makers have adequate and timely information to protect, utilize and enhance water resources. Several recurrent themes have emerged from the water resources planning process:

- Effective management solutions to water resource issues will be achieved only with the understanding that changes in environmental conditions are directly linked to socioeconomic patterns and processes, especially land use.
- Interactive partnerships among scientists, policy makers, and resource managers are essential for developing a comprehensive approach to integrating water sciences with management of water resources.
- Viewing water problems holistically and integrating research and management into a watershed context links the sciences involved in water research and management.
- The transfer of scientific information to regional/local leaders and the public should be done in a manner that will produce an informed and responsive citizenry, and
- Proposed recommendations are connected to issues that are related directly to societal needs, such as restoring and rehabilitating ecosystems, maintaining biodiversity, and understanding the effects of modified hydrologic flow.
- Climate change is an overarching challenge with potentially grim consequences to water resources managements.

Changes in NPS park planning standards (2004 *Park Planning Program Standards*) have re-framed park planning through six discrete elements of planning; the water planning process and its products are designed to integrate into this framework (Figure 2). Outside of this framework, the *Water Resources Information and Issues Overview Report* (not shown in Figure 2) is designed as a flexible document that addresses a park's specific needs with regard to water resources that are outside of the park planning framework. However, its contents may be used to support park planning efforts, particularly the General Management Plans and/or Program Management Plans. For the NHS, this *Water Resources Information and Issues Overview Report* is an important collation and summarization of water resource information, an identification of applicable federal, state, and local legislation and policy that affect the management of water resources, an assessment of current water resource status, an identification and analysis of water resource issues, and an assessment of future actions or management directions.

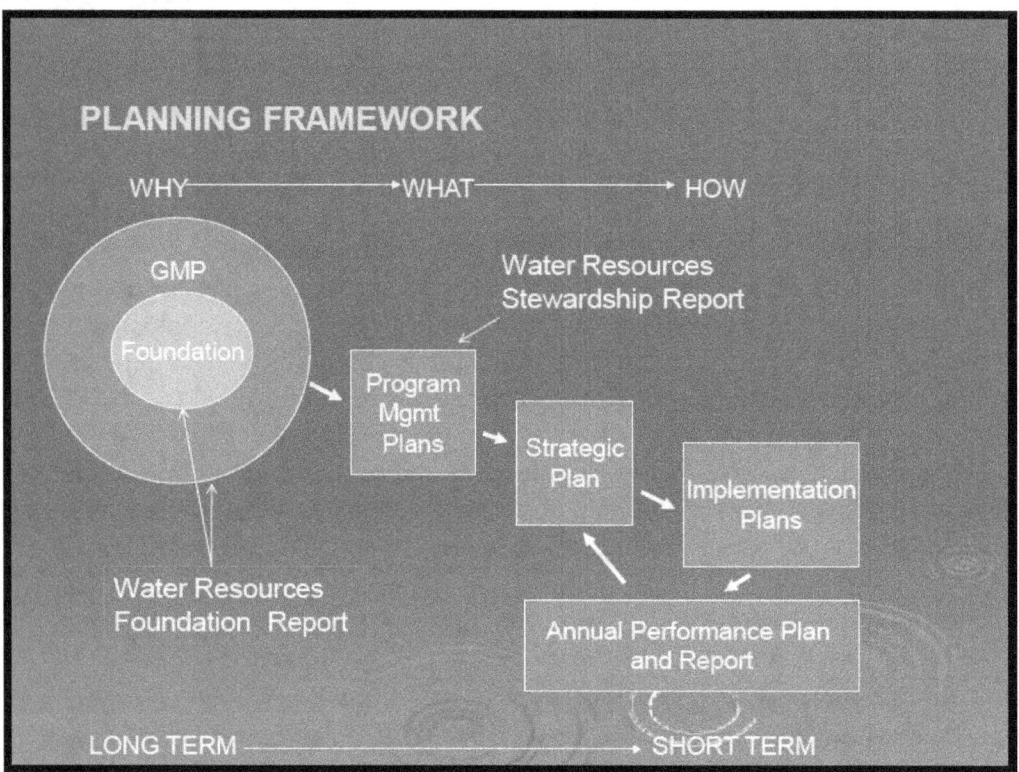

Figure 2. The NPS framework for planning and decision making (green boxes). Red-outlined boxes represent WRD planning documents. RSS = Resource Stewardship Strategy; GMP = General Management Plan.

Legislation, Management, and Coordination of Water Resources in Bent's Old Fort National Historic Site

Many federal, state, and local agencies have an interest, mandated or otherwise, in the water resources at the NHS. Protection of water resources requires an understanding of the various policy, regulatory, and management designations in order to facilitate coordination and cooperation among agencies and private landowners at the NHS. Both federal and state agencies have authority for the enforcement of appropriate regulations. Water resource laws and regulations at the state and local levels are often patterned after federal laws, or serve in response to federal directives.

Federal Laws and Regulations

National Park Service Organic Act of 1916: This act created the NPS and includes a significant management provision stating that the NPS *shall promote and regulate the use of the federal areas known as national parks, monuments, and reservations by such means and measures as conform to the fundamental purpose of the said parks, monuments, and reservations, which*

4

purpose is to conserve the scenery and the natural and historic objects and the wild life therein and to provide for the enjoyment of the same in such manner and by such means as will leave them unimpaired for future generations. The Organic Act also authorizes the NPS to *regulate the use* of national parks and develop rules, regulations and detailed policies to implement the broad policies provided by Congress. Rules and regulations for the national park system are described in the *Code of Federal Regulations* (Title 36).

General Authorities Act of 1970: This Act reinforced the 1916 Organic Act – all park lands are united by a common preservation purpose, regardless of title or designation. Hence, federal law protects all water resources in the national park system equally, and it is the fundamental duty of the NPS to protect those resources unless otherwise indicated by Congress.

Redwood National Park Act (1978): This Act amended the General Authorities Act of 1970 identifying the *high public value and integrity of the national park system* as reason to manage and protect all park system units. The act further stated that no activities should be allowed that will compromise the *values and purposes for which these various areas have been established*, except where specifically authorized by law or provided for by Congress.

National Parks Omnibus Management Act of 1998: This Act attempts to improve the ability of the NPS to provide state-of-the-art management, protection, and interpretation of and research on the resources of the national park system by:

- Assuring that management of units of the national park system is enhanced by the availability and utilization of a broad program of the highest quality science and information;

- Authorizing the establishment of cooperative agreements with colleges and universities, including but not limited to land grant schools, in partnership with other federal and state agencies, to establish cooperative study units to conduct multi-disciplinary research and develop integrated information products on the resources of the national park system, or of the larger region of which parks are a part;

- Undertaking a program of inventory and monitoring of national park system resources to establish baseline information and to provide information on the long-term trends in the condition of national park system resources; and

- Taking such measures as are necessary to assure the full and proper utilization of the results of scientific study for park management decisions. In each case in which an action undertaken by the NPS may cause a significant adverse effect on a park resource, the administrative record shall reflect the manner in which unit resource studies have been considered. The trend in the condition of resources of the national park system shall be a significant factor in the annual performance.

National Environmental Policy Act (NEPA) of 1969: This Act requires federal agencies to evaluate the environmental impacts of their actions and to integrate such evaluations into their decision-making processes. NEPA's basic policy is to assure that all branches of government give proper consideration to the environment prior to undertaking any major federal action that significantly affects the environment.

Clean Water Act of 1972 (Federal Water Pollution Control Act): The Federal Water Pollution Control Act, more commonly known as the Clean Water Act, was first promulgated in 1972 and amended several times since (e.g., 1977, 1987, and 1990). This law is designed to restore and maintain the chemical, physical and biological integrity of the nation's waters, including the waters of the national park system. To achieve this, the act called for a major grant program to assist in the construction of municipal sewage treatment facilities, and a program of effluent limitations designed to limit the amount of pollutants that could be discharged. Effluent limitations are the basis for permits issued for all point source discharges, known as the National Pollutant Discharge Elimination System (NPDES).

As part of the act, Congress recognized the primary role of the states in managing and regulating the nation's water quality. Section 313 requires that all federal agencies comply with the requirements of state law for water quality management, regardless of other jurisdictional status or landownership. States implement the protection of water quality under the authority granted by the Clean Water Act through best management practices and through water quality standards. Standards are based on the designated uses of a water body or segment of water, the water quality criteria necessary to protect that use or uses, and an anti-degradation provision to protect the existing water quality.

Section 303 of the Clean Water Act requires the promulgation of water quality standards by the states. Additionally, each state is required to review its water quality standards at least once every three years. This section also requires the listing of those waters where effluent limitations are not stringent enough to implement any water quality standard [so called 303(d) list]. Each state must establish Total Maximum Daily Loads (TMDLs) for applicable pollutants for each of the waters on its 303 (d) list.

Section 404 of the Clean Water Act requires that a permit be issued for discharge of dredged or fill materials in waters of the U.S., including wetlands. The U.S. Army Corps of Engineers administers the Section 404 permit program with oversight and veto powers held by the U.S. Environmental Protection Agency. Under Section 401, the State must certify that any 404 action meets current state water quality standards.

The 1987 amendment to the Clean Water Act established a stringent nonpoint source control mandate. Subsequent amendments further developed this mandate by requiring that states develop regulatory controls over nonpoint sources of pollution and over storm water runoff from industrial, municipal, and construction activities.

Endangered Species Act of 1973: This 1973 Act requires the NPS to identify and promote the conservation of all federally listed endangered, threatened, or candidate species within any park unit boundary. This Act requires all entities using federal funding to consult with the Secretary of Interior on activities that potentially impact endangered flora and fauna. It also requires agencies to protect endangered and threatened species, as well as designated critical habitats. While not required by legislation, it is NPS policy to also identify state and locally listed species of concern and support the preservation and restoration of those species and their habitats.

Safe Drinking Water Act of 1974: This is the primary federal legislation (1974 with amendments in 1986 and 1996) protecting drinking water supplied by public water systems (those serving more than 25 people). The act provides for the establishment of primary regulations for the protection of the public health and secondary regulations relating to the taste, odor, and appearance of drinking water. The law established the current federal-state arrangement in which states may be delegated primary implementation and enforcement authority for the drinking water program; the 1986 amendments sought to accelerate contaminant regulation. The state-administered Public Water Supply Supervision (PWSS) program remains the basic program for regulating the Nation's public water systems.

The 2006 NPS Management Policies cover water supply systems, wastewater systems, and recreational waters. Specific guidance is provided by Director's Order 83: Public Health and its associated Reference Manuals – 83A1 (Drinking Water Standards); 83A2 (Cross Connection Control); 83A3 (Water System Security); 93B1 (Wastewater Systems); and 83B4 (Sewage Spill Response Notification).

Rivers and Harbors Act of 1899: Section 9 of this Act prohibits the construction of any bridge, dam, dike or causeway over or in navigable waterways of the U.S. without Congressional approval. Administration of section 9 has been delegated to the Coast Guard. Structures authorized by state legislatures may be built if the affected navigable waters are totally within one state, provided that the plan is approved by the Corps of Engineers and the Secretary of Army.

Under section 10 of the Act, structures of the United States cannot obstruct navigation without Congressional authorization. Plans for structures or fill in waters of the United States require approval by the Secretary of the Army through the Corps of Engineers.

Authority of the Corps of Engineers to issue permits for the discharge of refuse matter into or affecting navigable waters under section 13 was modified by the Federal Water Pollution Control Act Amendments of 1972, as amended, which established National Pollutant Discharge Elimination System Permits.

Fish and Wildlife Coordination Act of 1934: The Fish and Wildlife Coordination Act, as amended, provides authority for the U.S. Fish and Wildlife Service to review and comment on the effects on fish and wildlife of activities proposed to be undertaken or permitted by the Corps of Engineers.

Amendments enacted in 1946 require consultation with the U.S. Fish and Wildlife Service and the fish and wildlife agencies of states where the "waters of any stream or other body of water are proposed or authorized, permitted or licensed to be impounded, diverted . . . or otherwise controlled or modified" by any agency under a federal permit or license. Consultation is to be undertaken for the purpose of "preventing loss of and damage to wildlife resources."

The 1958 amendments added provisions to recognize the vital contribution of wildlife resources to the Nation and to require equal consideration and coordination of wildlife conservation with other water resources development programs. The amendments also expanded the instances in which diversions or modifications to water bodies would require consultation with the U.S. Fish and Wildlife Service.

Executive Order 11990: Wetlands Protection: This executive order directs the NPS to 1) provide leadership and to take action to minimize the destruction, loss, or degradation of wetlands, 2) preserve and enhance the natural and beneficial values of wetlands, and 3) to avoid direct or indirect support of new construction in wetlands unless there are no practicable alternative to such construction and the proposed action includes all practicable measures to minimize harm to wetlands.

Executive Order 11988: Floodplain Management: This executive order requires all federal agencies to take action to reduce the risk of flood loss, to restore and preserve the natural and beneficial values served by floodplains, and to minimize the impact of floods on human safety, health, and welfare. The objective of this executive order is "…to avoid to the extent possible the long- and short-term adverse impacts associated with the occupancy and modification of floodplains and to avoid direct and indirect support of floodplain development wherever there is a practicable alternative." For non-repetitive actions, the executive order states that all proposed facilities must be located outside the limits of the 100-year floodplain. If there were no practicable alternative to construction within the floodplain, adverse impacts would be minimized during the design of the project.

Executive Order 13112: Invasive Species: This executive order requires the prevention of the introduction of invasive species and provides for their control and minimization of the economic, ecological, and human health impacts that invasive species cause. It complements and builds upon existing federal authority to aid in the prevention and control of invasive species.

State of Colorado Laws and Regulations

Colorado Revised Statutes, Title 25 (Health), Article 8 (Water Quality Control): This Article provides for the development and maintenance of water quality standards in Colorado and the prevention, abatement, and control of water pollution. Commonly referred to as the Colorado Water Quality Control Act, this article is administered by the Water Quality Control Commission, the state agency responsible for promulgating rules and regulations to govern water quality. Important regulations include:

- Regulation No. 32 – Classifications and Numeric Standards for the Arkansas River Basin and Tables;
- Regulation No. 93 – Colorado's Section 303(d) List of Impaired Waters and Monitoring and Evaluation List;
- Regulation No. 41– The Basic Standards for Ground Water
- Regulation No. 42 – Site-Specific Water Quality Classification and Standards for Ground Water
- Regulation No. 82 – 401 Certification Regulation

- Primary Drinking Water Regulations – 5 CCR 1003-1

Colorado Revised Statutes, Title 33 (Wildlife and Parks and Outdoor Recreation), Articles 1-8 (Wildlife): These Articles cover the conservation, protection, and enforcement rules for game and nongame wildlife. Article 2 covers nongame and endangered species conservation as it pertains to the two state-listed nongame fish species that occur in the NHS.

Colorado Revised Statutes, Title 37 (Water and Irrigation), Articles 1-8 (Flood Control), Articles 60 (Colorado Water Conservation Board), Article 69 (Arkansas River Compact), and Articles 80-92 (Water Rights and Irrigation): Articles 80-92 are on particular importance to the NHS because they cover Colorado water rights law. The doctrine of prior appropriation governs the establishment and administration of ground water rights in Colorado. Ground water in Colorado is subject to a complex administration scheme. All ground water is presumed by law to be tributary to a surface stream; based on that presumption ground water is governed by the prior appropriation doctrine and administered in conjunction with surface water rights. Such waters are administered through the state's water courts. The state recognizes that not all ground water is hydrologically connected to surface streams and provides for administration of such nontributary ground waters separately from surface streams, providing different schemes based on the degree of hydrologic connection and areal location within the state.

National Park Service Policies and Director's Orders

The NPS Management Policies (National Park Service 2006) provide broad policy guidance for the management of National Park System units. These NPS policies and guidelines broadly require management of natural resources of the National Park System to maintain, rehabilitate, and perpetuate the inherent integrity of aquatic resources. Section 4.6 of the management policies specifically addresses water resource management including protection of surface waters and ground water, water rights, water quality, floodplains, wetlands, and watershed and stream processes. It is NPS policy to determine the quality of park surface and ground water resources and avoid, whenever feasible, the pollution of park waters by human activities occurring within and outside of parks. Specifically, the NPS works with appropriate governmental bodies to: achieve the highest possible standards available under the Clean Water Act for protection of park waters, take all actions necessary to maintain or restore surface and ground water quality within the parks to be in compliance with the Clean Water Act and all applicable laws and regulations, and develop agreements with other governing bodies, where appropriate, to obtain their cooperation in maintaining or restoring the quality of park water resources. NPS Management Policies also direct the NPS to: manage watersheds as complete hydrologic systems, minimize human disturbance to natural upland processes that deliver water, sediment, and woody debris to streams, and manage streams to protect stream processes that create habitat features, including floodplains, riparian systems, woody debris accumulations, terraces, gravel bars, riffles, and pools.

In accordance with these management policies, the NPS will protect watershed and stream features mainly by avoiding impacts to watershed and riparian vegetation and allowing natural fluvial processes to proceed unimpeded. When conflicts between park infrastructure and stream processes are unavoidable, park managers will first consider relocating or redesigning infrastructure, instead of manipulating streams. However, where stream manipulation is inevitable, the NPS will use techniques that protect natural processes to the greatest extent practicable. In addition, the NPS will allow natural shoreline processes to continue without interference. Where human uses or infrastructure have altered the nature or rate of natural shoreline processes, the NPS will investigate alternatives for mitigating such effects.

Director's Orders (DO) and Procedural Manuals: National Park Service DO's and procedural manuals describe the recommended procedures for implementing service-wide policy. Those DO's and procedural manuals that pertain most directly to water resources are described below.

- DO #77-1 and Procedural Manual #77-1: Wetland Protection: The purpose of DO #77-1 is to establish NPS policies, requirements, and standards for implementing Executive Order 11990, *Protection of Wetlands* (42 FR 26961). The NPS adopts a goal of "no net loss of wetlands." In addition, the NPS will strive to achieve a longer-term goal of net gain of wetlands service-wide. DO #77-1 directs NPS units to conduct park-wide wetland inventories to help assure proper planning with respect to management and protection of wetland resources and sets forth the standard for defining, classifying, and inventorying wetlands. For proposed new development or other new activities or programs that are either located in or otherwise have the potential for adverse impacts on wetlands, the NPS will employ a sequence of: 1) avoiding adverse wetland impacts to the extent practicable, 2) minimizing impacts that could not be avoided, and 3) compensating for remaining unavoidable adverse wetland impacts via restoration of degraded wetlands. Where natural wetland characteristics or functions have been degraded or lost due to previous or ongoing human activities, the NPS will, to the extent appropriate and practicable, restore them to pre-disturbance conditions. Where appropriate and practicable, the NPS will not simply protect, but will seek to enhance natural wetland values by using them for educational, recreational, scientific, and similar purposes that do not disrupt natural wetland functions. A Wetland Statement of Findings (WSOF) must be completed in accordance with procedures described in Procedural Manual #77-1 (Wetland Protection), when any NPS wetlands are adversely impacted. Procedural manual #77-1 provides more detailed procedures by which the NPS will implement DO #77-1.

  According to the 2006 *NPS Management Policies*, the NPS will manage wetlands in compliance with NPS mandates and the requirements of Executive Order 11990 (Wetland Protection), the Clean Water Act, and the Rivers and Harbors Appropriation Act of 1899, and the procedures described in Director's Order 77-1. The service will 1) provide leadership and take action to prevent the destruction, loss, and degradation of wetlands; 2) preserve and enhance the natural and beneficial values of wetlands; and 3) avoid direct and indirect support of new construction in wetlands unless there are no practicable alternatives and the proposed action includes all practicable measures to minimize harm to wetlands. The NPS will implement a "no net loss of wetlands" policy.

- DO #77-2 and Procedural Manual #77-2: Floodplain Management: DO #77-2 applies to all proposed NPS actions involving floodplain development that could adversely affect the natural resources and functions of floodplains or increase flood risks. In compliance with Executive Order 11988, *Floodplain Management*, it is NPS policy to preserve floodplain values and minimize potentially hazardous conditions associated with flooding. Specifically, DO #77-2 directs the NPS to:

- o protect and preserve the natural resources and functions of floodplains;
- o avoid the long- and short-term environmental effects associated with the occupancy and modification of floodplains;
- o avoid support of floodplain development and actions that could adversely affect the natural resources and functions of floodplains or increase flood risks; and
- o restore, when practicable, natural floodplain values previously affected by land use activities within floodplains.

When it is not practicable to locate or relocate development or inappropriate human activities to a site outside and not affecting the floodplain, NPS will:

- o prepare and approve a Floodplain Statement of Findings, in accordance with procedures described in Procedural Manual #77-2;
- o take all reasonable actions to minimize the impact to natural resources of floodplains;
- o use non-structural measures as much as practicable to reduce hazards to human life and property; and
- o ensure that structures and facilities are designed to be consistent with the intent of the standards and criteria of the National Flood Insurance Program (44 CFR Part 60).

Procedural Manual #77-2 establishes NPS procedures for implementing floodplain protection and management actions for national park system units in accordance with DO #77-2. The manual defines regulatory floodplains and the information required to delineate floodplains, defines the information required to evaluate hazards associated with the modification or occupation of floodplains, and provides requirements for managing activities that impact floodplains.

The *2006 NPS Management Policies* state that natural shoreline processes (such as erosion, deposition, dune formation, shoreline migration) will be allowed to continue without interference. Where human activities have altered the nature or rate of natural shoreline processes, the NPS will, in consultation with appropriate state and federal agencies, investigate alternatives for mitigating the effects of such activities or structures and for restoring natural conditions. New developments will not be placed in areas subject to wave erosion or active shoreline processes unless 1) the development is required by law; or 2) the development is essential to meet the parks' purposes, as defined by its establishing act of proclamation, and

- o No practicable alternative locations are available,
- o The development will be reasonably assured of surviving during its planned life span, without the need for shoreline control measures, and
- o Steps will be taken to minimize safety hazards and harm to property and natural resources.

- DO#35A: Sale or Lease of Park Services, Resources or Water in Support of Activities Outside the Boundaries of National Park Areas: Neither the law or NPS policy obligates the NPS to sell or lease any services, resources or water. While this DO conditionally allows the NPS to authorize the sale or lease of water, the NPS's primary responsibility under the Organic Act is the preservation and protection of park resources -- and the water dependent environment – for the enjoyment of future generations. Under this DO, park superintendents may exercise the Director's authority to sell or lease park services, resources or water, provided that the requirements contained in the DO are met; and, the NPS will consider a request for use of park services, resources or water through a special use permit application and approval process, or through the use of a written agreement.

- Reference Manual #77: Natural Resource Management: Reference Manual #77 offers comprehensive guidance to NPS employees responsible for managing, conserving, and protecting the natural resources found in national park system units. The Manual serves as the primary guidance on implementing Service-wide natural resource management in units of the national park system. Specific natural resources pertaining to water addressed in the manual include the management, protection, and use of: fish and fishery resources, freshwater resources, marine resources, nonnative species, shorelines, and marine, freshwater, and barrier island resources.

Management Agencies

Management of the Arkansas River and associated waters within and adjacent to the NHS involves several federal and state agencies.

U. S. Army Corps of Engineers (ACOE): The ACOE serves the American public in the areas of environmental enhancement, navigation, flood damage reduction, water and wetlands regulation, recreation sites, and disaster response. The agency issues permits for the placement of structures, dredging and filling of navigable waters under Section 10 of the Rivers and Harbors Act. It also regulates the discharge of dredged or other fill into all waters of the U. S. under Section 404, Clean Water Act. No section 404 permit may be issued by the ACOE without a section 401 certification from the Colorado Department of Public Health and the Environment stating that the discharge of dredged or fill material will not violate state water quality standards.

The ACOE also has enforcement authority to prohibit placement of any refuse or debris in a river or on the bank that may be washed into the river and obstruct navigation (Sec. 13, Rivers and Harbor Act).

U. S. Fish and Wildlife Service (USFWS): The Fish and Wildlife Coordination Act of 1934 mandates that all federal agencies consult with the USFWS on permit and license applications involving water development projects. Section 7 of the Endangered Species Act mandates that all federal agencies consult with the USFWS to ensure that actions do not jeopardize federally listed species.

U.S. Environmental Protection Agency (EPA): The EPA establishes standards for water quality management, drinking water safety, solid and hazardous waste disposal, toxic substance management, air quality control and general environmental quality review. Most enforcement is delegated to the states with EPA oversight. The EPA may veto a 404 permit, and it may initiate the lead federal role for certain cases. In Colorado the primary enforcement role for water quality is filled by the Colorado Department of Public Health and the Environment.

U.S. Geological Survey (USGS): The USGS is primarily responsible for collecting data on natural resources and the physical environment. This includes information on geological and biological resources, water resources, maps and mapping, and earthquakes and other natural disasters.

Natural Resources Conservation Service (NRCS): The NRCS provides technical and financial assistance to help agricultural producers and others care for the land. NRCS helps landowners develop conservation plans, conducts soil surveys, and conservation needs assessments. Specific Colorado Programs include grassland reserve, emergency watershed protection, small watershed, wetlands reserve, and wildlife habitat incentive. The La Junta, CO Area 3 office of the NRCS serves southeastern Colorado. The NRCS is developing Rapid Watershed Assessments (RWAs) to provide natural resource snapshots and overviews of each of Colorado's 8-digit Hydrologic Unit Codes. A RWA was developed in 2007 (NRCS 2007) for the Upper Arkansas-Lake Meredith watershed (HUC 11020005) where the NHS resides (http://www.co.nrcs.usda.gov/technical/WaterRes/LakeMerdithRWA.html).

Colorado Department of Public Health and the Environment (CDPHE): The Department oversees the protection of the state's waters and is charged with conserving the state's waters and protecting, maintaining, and improving their quality for the wildlife and aquatic life for domestic, agricultural, industrial, recreational, and other beneficial uses. The Water Quality Control Commission (WQCC) is the administrative agency responsible for developing specific state water quality policies. The WQCC adopts water quality classifications and standards for surface and ground waters of the state, as well as various regulations aimed at achieving compliance with those classifications and standards. The Water Quality Division of the CDPHE serves as staff to the Commission and provides them with recommendations based on assessment of the state's waters. Within the Department of Natural Resources, the Division of Water Resources, headed by the State Engineer, ensures the competent distribution of water, and administers water rights through the appropriation doctrine. This division also controls permits for ground water wells, provides water supply statistics, and surface flow data.

The state notes nine designated uses of water including two levels each for Aquatic Cold Water and Warm Water, domestic water supply, and three different uses for Recreation and Agriculture. Colorado does not have a list of Tier III waters (highest water quality and protection), but instead refers to them as Outstanding Waters. The State has no stream flow or biological criteria or guidance with which to protect existing uses.

Colorado Water Conservation Board (CWCB): The CWCB represents each major water basin, Denver, and other state agencies in a joint effort to use water wisely and protect Colorado water for future generations. The CWCB consists of 15 members. Eight voting members represent the state's major water basins, including the Arkansas River. Services and programs of the CWCB include, among many, grants, loans, technical assistance (e.g., water conservation planning, drought mitigation planning, mapping and GIS), stream flow monitoring, floodplain mapping, instream flow, and salinity control. The CWCB ensures the development, protection, and management of Colorado's waters. It is the only entity that can hold an instream water right.

Colorado Division of Wildlife: The Division of Wildlife manages the state's wildlife species. It regulates hunting and fishing activities by issuing licenses and enforcing regulations. The Division also manages more than 230 wildlife areas for public recreation, conducts research to improve wildlife management activities, provides technical assistance to private and other public landowners concerning wildlife and habitat management, and develops programs to protect and recover threatened and endangered species. Colorado statutes require the Division to operate under the jurisdiction of the Colorado Wildlife Commission. The Commission is responsible for all wildlife management, for licensing requirements, and for the promulgation of rules, regulations, and orders concerning wildlife programs. It also establishes broad, long-term policy statements that provide direction to the Division for purposes of managing wildlife resources in Colorado.

Colorado Division of Water Resources: Ground water administration and enforcement is one of the primary responsibilities of the Division of Water Resources, led by the State Engineer. The State Engineer also provides staff to assist in technical support to the Colorado Ground Water Commission, in the exercise of its duties in the designated basins, generally located on the eastern plains of Colorado. Well permits for wells in these basins are evaluated by the staff of the State Engineer based on Commission rules.

The Division is empowered to administer all water rights according to the Appropriation Doctrine (in short, 1st in time, 1st in right). This includes releasing water from reservoirs to satisfy senior water users in Colorado and meeting the obligations to Kansas under the Arkansas River Compact. Most of this work is done by Division offices located in the seven major river basins of the state. These offices employ water commissioners to ensure the priority system is followed, enforcing the decrees and water laws of the State of Colorado. The Colorado Ground Water Law established the permitting requirement of ground water wells, and by 1969, surface and ground water rights were administered together.

Stakeholders at the Local Level

Arkansas River Basin Water Forum: The Forum, first held in 1995, was developed as a means to bring together the diverse water interests to explain their views and engage in open dialogue about water resource issues in the basin. Through this dialogue the Forum seeks to find common ground between primary water users in the basin.

Southeast Colorado Resource Conservation and Development Council: This non-profit organization works with local units of government, community organizations, groups, and individuals to coordinate technical and financial assistance to meet the needs of the local area. The vision of the council is to have an active, progressive network of communities working together for the good of all citizens through creative projects and activities that develop the regional economy, enhance our environment, and preserve our heritage. The council concentrates on areas of land management, water management, land conservation, and community development. The council recently developed a *Lower Arkansas Watershed Plan* (Tetra Tech 2007; see below).

Southeast Colorado Water Conservancy District: The Southeastern Colorado Water Conservancy District was created under Colorado State Statutes in 1958 for the purpose of developing and administering the Fryingpan-Arkansas Project. The District extends along the Arkansas River from Buena Vista to Lamar, and along Fountain Creek from Colorado Springs to Pueblo. The District is the legal agency responsible for repayment of the reimbursable costs of the project. In addition to administering this repayment responsibility, the District makes supplemental water from the Fryingpan-Arkansas Project available for use on irrigated land under various private and mutual ditch companies, and for use by municipal and domestic water suppliers who directly serve the District's approximately constituents.

Lower Arkansas Valley Water Conservancy District: In November 2002, voters in Pueblo, Otero, Crowley, Bent and Prowers counties approved an initiative to form the Lower Arkansas Valley Water Conservancy District. The Board of Directors was appointed that December, and the new District held its first meeting. The mission of the district is to acquire, retain and conserve water flowing in the Arkansas River and its tributaries; to insure that all water will remain in the valley for socioeconomic benefit of the District citizens; and to participate in water-related projects that will embody thoughtful conservation, responsible growth, and beneficial water usage within the Lower Arkansas Valley.

Colorado Water Protective and Development Association (CWPDA): CWPDA is a 501-C12 non-profit organization, incorporated in the State of Colorado in 1965. The stated primary purpose of the association is to protect and develop underground and surface waters of the Arkansas River Basin. CWPDA has approximately 600 members, including the NHS, representing approximately 1336 wells. The NHS pays fees to the CWPDA to include its wells in the Association. The membership is composed of individuals, corporations, municipalities, and other entities that own or control wells within the Arkansas River Basin. CWPDA's municipal members provide water to about 38,000 people and irrigation wells of its members provided sole source and supplemental irrigation water to over 71,000 acres. CWPDA municipal members are primarily the agricultural communities between Fowler and Las Animas.

Arkansas River Watershed Invasive Plant Plan (ARKWIPP): ARKWIPP was founded with the mission to offer landowners and land managers reliable information regarding invasive plants such as tamarisk and viable ways in which to join the control and restoration process in the Arkansas River Basin. The working goal of this group is a restored Arkansas River riparian ecosystem. The NHS is member of this group.

Related Management Plans and Programs
Tetra Tech (2007) developed the *Lower Arkansas Watershed Plan* for the Southeast Colorado Resource Conservation and Development Council in Lamar, CO. The planning process was a cooperative effort and the NHS is a stakeholder/partner in this plan. The plan recognizes the agricultural and recreational history of the lower Arkansas River watershed, and the vast canal systems that have diverted and distributed water of the Arkansas River in the seven-county region for over a hundred years. In doing so, this plan's focus is on identification of water quality issues and reducing pollutants through identification and implementation of management strategies and solutions. The plan's vision is to develop the blueprint that will integrate watershed goals for sustainable community and agricultural development, water supply, fisheries, habitat preservation, flood control and recreation, and wildlife habitat to support water

quality improvement in the Lower Arkansas River basin. Four goals and a number of measurable objectives to achieve the goals support that vision.

Bent's Old Fort NHS is one of 11 park units that comprised the Southern Plains Inventory and Monitoring Network (SOPN), one of 32 similar networks nationwide. These inventory and monitoring networks are part of an effort in the National Park Service to develop a stronger scientific basis for stewardship and management of natural resources across the national park system. A large part of this scientific basis is the development of vital signs. Vital signs are a subset of physical, chemical, and biological elements and processes of park ecosystems that are selected to represent the overall health or condition of a park's natural resources, known or hypothesized effects of stressors, or elements that have important human values. They are the key elements that indicate the health of an ecosystem. Vital signs can be any feature of the environment that can be measured or estimated and that provide insights into the state of the ecosystem.

The SOPN has identified 11 vital signs for the network park units, four of which have importance to water resources: ground water levels; surface water quantity and water quality; wetland vegetation communities; and early detection of exotic plants (http://science.nature.nps.gov/im/units/sopn/monitoring.cfm). Texas State University (2007) recommended monitoring activities with regard to ground water, surface water quantity, and surface water quality for the NHS. No specific recommendations to the NHS have been made with regard to wetland vegetation communities and early detection of exotic plants.

Description of Resources

Climate

The climate of southeastern Colorado is semiarid -- many years are drier than average and some years receive only half or less the long-term average for precipitation. The region of short-grass prairie seems almost always in or on the verge of drought, and multi-year droughts occur on a 10-20 year cycle (Perkins *et al.* 2005a,b). Some of the worst multi-year droughts occurred in the 1930s, mid-1950s, 1970s and early 2000s. The climate is characterized by low relative humidity, abundant sunshine, infrequent rains and snow, moderate to high wind movement, and a large daily and seasonal range in temperature. Hot, dry summers contribute to dry soils and the potential for soil erosion. Rainfall occurs as frontal storms in the spring and early summer and high intensity, convective thunderstorms occur in late summer; such rainfall is frequently limited to a small geographical area. However, much of the area is more directly dependent on mountain-based snowfall and storage than on rainfall.

From 1982-2005, the annual, average maximum and minimum temperatures for La Junta were 70.8° F and 39.2° F, respectively (Table 1). From June to August the average maximum temperature is 91° F while the average minimum temperature from December to February is 15° F. For the same period of record, the annual precipitation averaged approximately 15.3 inches (Table 1). An important feature of the precipitation is its seasonality; approximately, 70 percent of the precipitation falls during April-October and only 10 percent falls from November-February. Evaporation during the growing season (April-October) exceeds precipitation, thus irrigation of crops is needed.

Table 1. Monthly climate summary for the La Junta, CO station (#054726) from 1982-2005 (from http://www.wrcc.dri.edu).

	Jan	Feb	Mar	Apr	May	Jun	Jul	Aug	Sep	Oct	Nov	Dec	Annual
Average Max. Temperature (°F)	49.3	52.3	60.3	68.9	78.8	89.2	95.1	92.4	84.4	72.3	57.6	48.7	70.8
Average Min. Temperature (°F)	18.0	21.0	29.1	37.3	48.2	57.7	63.5	61.8	52.1	37.4	26.3	17.7	39.2
Average Total Precipitation (in.)	0.48	0.49	1.26	1.68	2.06	1.71	2.46	1.97	0.97	1.00	0.74	0.45	15.29
Average Total Snow Fall (in.)	4.4	4.3	4.6	2.2	0.4	0.0	0.0	0.0	0.2	1.5	3.6	5.1	26.3
Average Snow Depth (in.)	1	1	0	0	0	0	0	0	0	0	0	1	0

Land Use

Irrigation and floodplain soils in the lower Arkansas River valley have resulted in some of the most productive agricultural lands in Colorado for growing onions, cantaloupe, watermelons, peppers, tomatoes, cucumbers, alfalfa, corn and wheat. Beyond the valley floor, the watershed turns to short grass prairie with the major form of land use being livestock production.

The majority of land surrounding the NHS is zoned as agricultural, with some portions rowcropped and others grazed (NPS 2005). The eastern boundary of the NHS is shared with a 400-acre state wildlife area with seasonal hunts and low intensity rowcropping. State Highway 194 forms the northern boundary while US 50 forms the southern boundary.

Approximately 483 acres within the NHS have been previously disturbed by either cattle grazing (primarily south of Arkansas River), irrigated crops (primarily north of Arkansas River), or impacted by fire and/or exotic plant species infestations prior to federal ownership. Sixty-eight acres on the north side have been restored to native grasses.

Visitor use of the NHS peaked in the late 1970s, dropped and stabilized from the early 1980s to late 1990s, and maintained approximately 30,000 annual visitors from 2000-2006 (Figure 3). A picnic area just inside the main park gate is currently available for daytime use. Response from visitor surveys conducted the past couple years indicates public interest in some type of overnight camping facility, either tent sites or RV parking, available in the park.

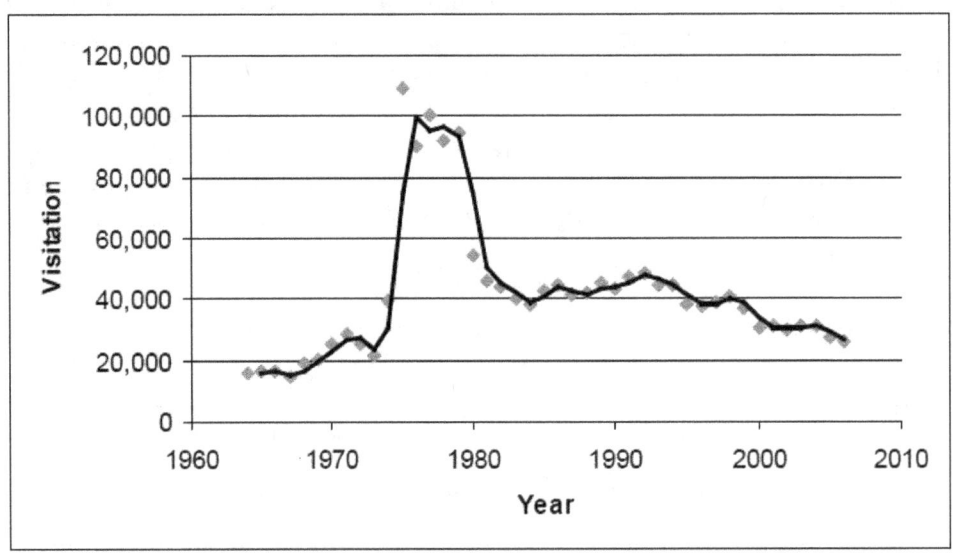

Figure 3. Average annual visitation in thousands for Bent's Old Fort National Historic Site, 1964-2006 (Bent's Old Fort NHS visitation statistics).

The NHS has two historic trails. The paved ¼-mile walkway leading from the visitor parking lot to the fort and an interpretive trail (1.4 mi loop) from the fort through the cottonwood grove, around a large wetland and back to the visitor parking lot. Visitor use is concentrated on the north side of the NHS.

The NHS lands south of the Arkansas River (approximately 450 acres) consist of the riparian area along the river and abandoned farmland. Presently, these lands are not developed for visitor use, and no official public access exists. A system of fire roads through this area is used by NHS resource management staff. There is a possibility of a developed trail from La Junta to this area of the NHS through a cooperative effort with local communities and the NPS Rivers, Trails and Conservation Assistance Program (Wallner 2006). Access for recreational activities along the Arkansas River, such as fishing and boating, are not available through the park. This lack of

18

public access is largely due to the river's classification as an Aquatic Life Warm Water - Class 2 waterway (Fran Pannebaker, Bent's Old Fort NHS, pers. comm. 2007). This class of waterway includes waters that are not capable of sustaining a wide variety of warm water biota, including sensitive species, due to physical habitat, water flows or levels, or uncorrectable water quality conditions that result in substantial impairment of the abundance and diversity of species.

Physiography, Geology, Soils, and Vegetation

The NHS lies in the Colorado Piedmont section of the Great Plains Physiographic Province (Fenneman and Johnson 1946). The Colorado Piedmont ranges in elevations from 3,975 ft at the point where the Arkansas River enters Bent County (immediately east of Otero County) to 5,200 ft north of Delhi, CO. Generally, the area around the NHS consists of flat to gently rolling surfaces with steep intervening slopes (NPS 2005). The NHS (4035 ft in elevation) includes an active floodplain and a series of stepped river terraces, shaped by the hydro-geomorphic effect of the Arkansas River.

Changes in channel gradient, discharge or sediment load can lead to a river channel incising its floodplain. The original floodplain is abandoned and is left as a relatively flat bench, known as a river terrace, which is separated from the new floodplain below a relatively steep slope (NPS 2005). Bent's Old Fort sits on such a terrace (Figure 4; elevation > 4000 ft).

NPS (2005), using Weist *et al.* (1965) as the source, mapped and described the rock units in the vicinity of NHS. The Bedrock of the NHS is the Bridge Creek Limestone, a member of the Greenhorn Limestone Formation. Readers should consult NPS (2005) for a detailed mapping and description of the structural geology of the NHS; however, NPS (2005) provided a less detailed map that describes the surficial geology of the NHS in terms of alluvium, terrace deposits, overbank fines, and saturated soil (see Figure 5); these are primarily alluvial deposits of Wisconsin age that are overlaid with more recent alluvial deposits (NPS 2005).

Soils in the NHS belong to the Rocky Ford-Numa-Kornman soil association that represents recent alluvial deposits (Stevens *et al.* 2007; Figure 6). These soils consist of deep, nearly level, well drained clay loam soils or silty-clay, sandy soils on river bottom lower plains. Bankard Sand occurs nearest to the river, deposited by flood waters (Figure 5). This sand is very well drained and supports cottonwoods, willows, and invasive tamarisk. The mature upper terrace exhibits a parent soil of thick, slit clay loam over a silt loam subsoil. The lower river terrace consists of nearly level, somewhat poorly drained, slightly saline, and clayey to sandy soils. The parent layer is about 12 inches thick and is generally high in organic matter. These soils are subject to occasional flooding. The subsoil is slowly permeable and poorly aerated. Salt tolerant plants, such as saltgrass (*Distichlis spicata*) and alkali sacaton (*Sporobolus airoides*), grow well on these soils.

The NHS is within the Great Plains – Palouse Steppe Ecological Province and the short-grass prairie ecoregion (NPS 2005). This part of the short-grass prairie ecoregion is dominated by buffalo grass (*Buchloe dactyloides*) and blue gramma grass (*Bouteloua gracilis*). The vegetation of the NHS is typical of lower Arkansas River valley (Figure 7). The banks of the river are lined with narrow bands of coyote willow (*Salix exigua*). The rest of the floodplain supports plains cottonwood (*Populus deltoides*) gallery forests with an understory of inland saltgrass (*D.*

19

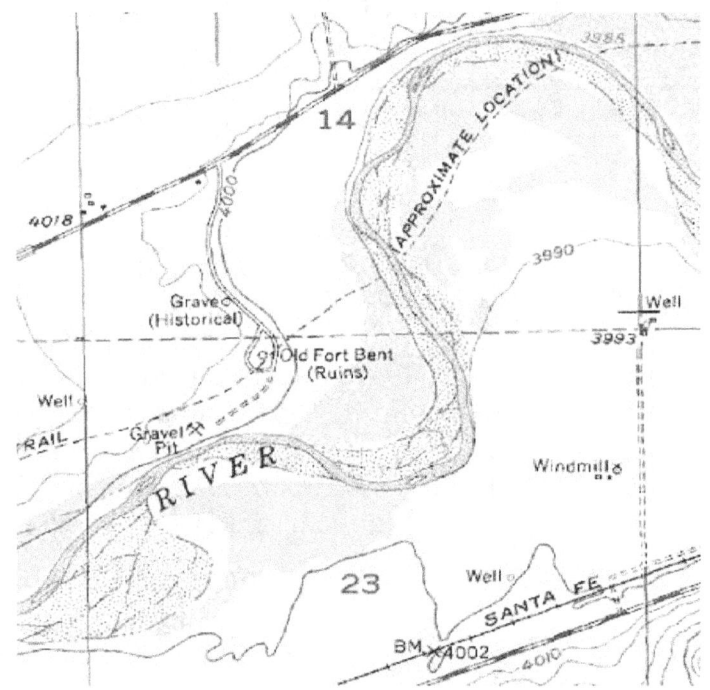

Figure 4. Aerial photograph (upper; circa 1993) and topographic map (lower; circa 1953) of Bent's Old Fort National Historic Site, showing the location of the fort on a river terrace.

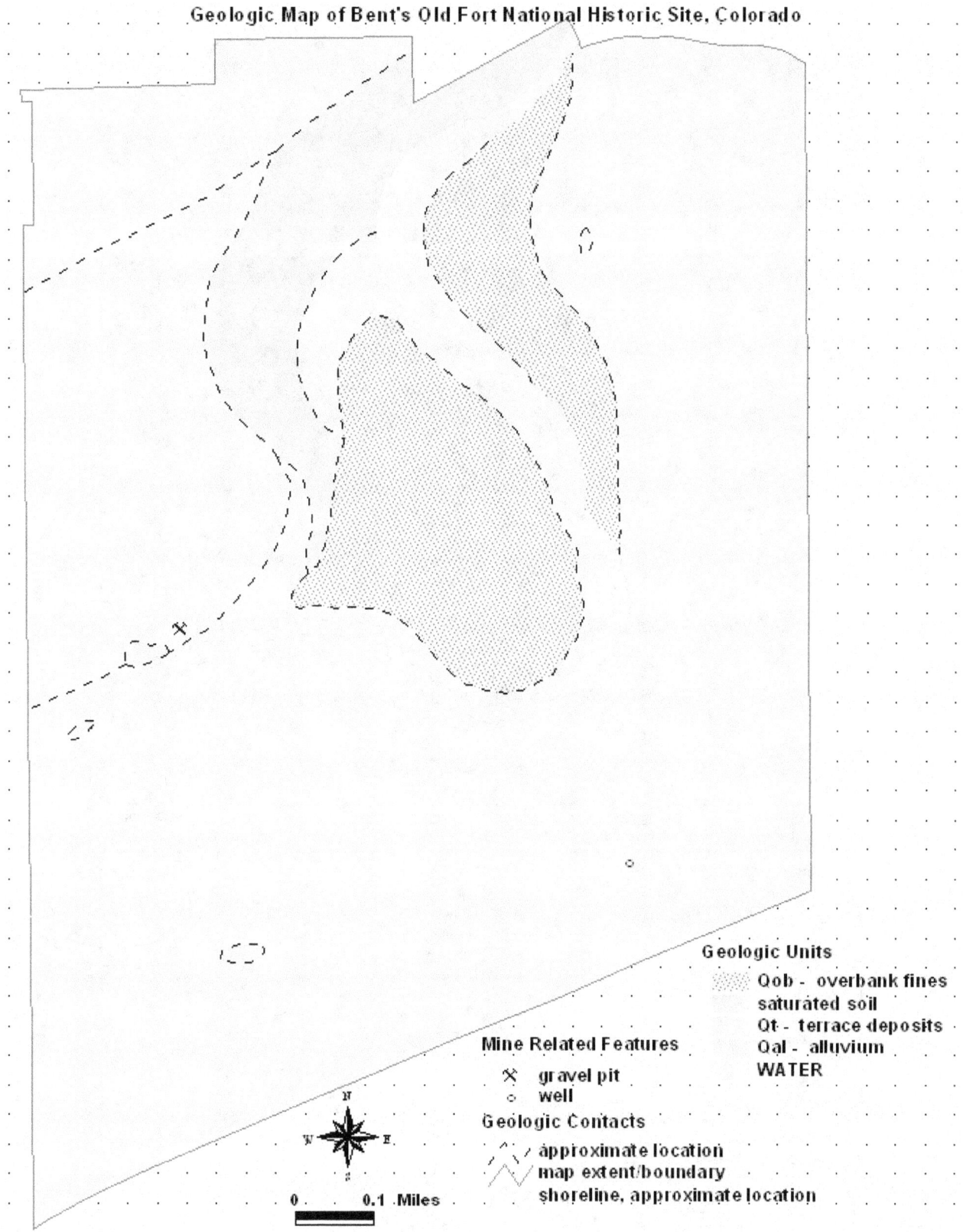

Figure 5. Surficial geology of Bent's Old Fort NHS (from NPS 2005).

21

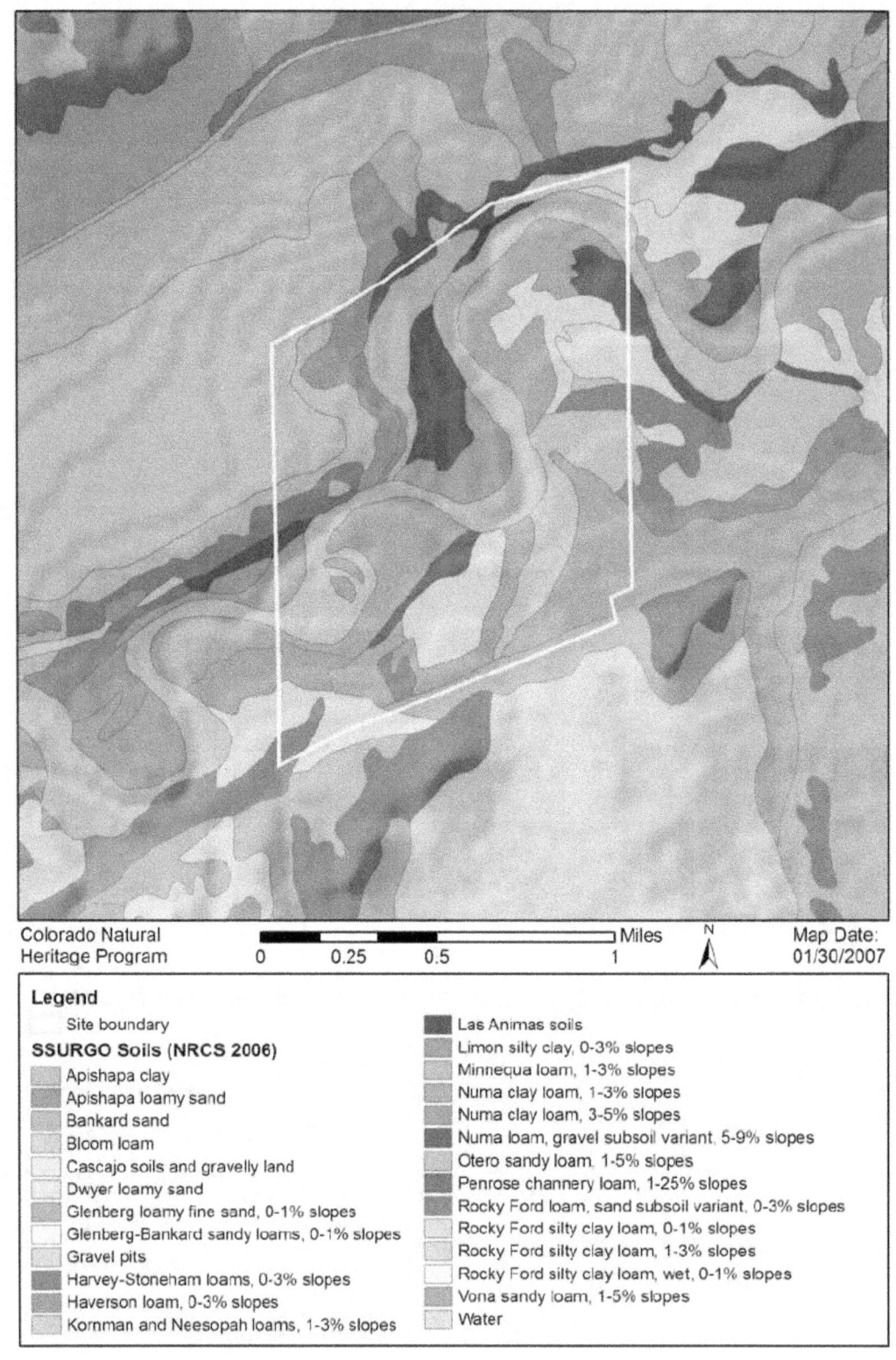

Figure 6. Soils of Bent's Old Fort NHS (from Stevens *et al.* 2007).

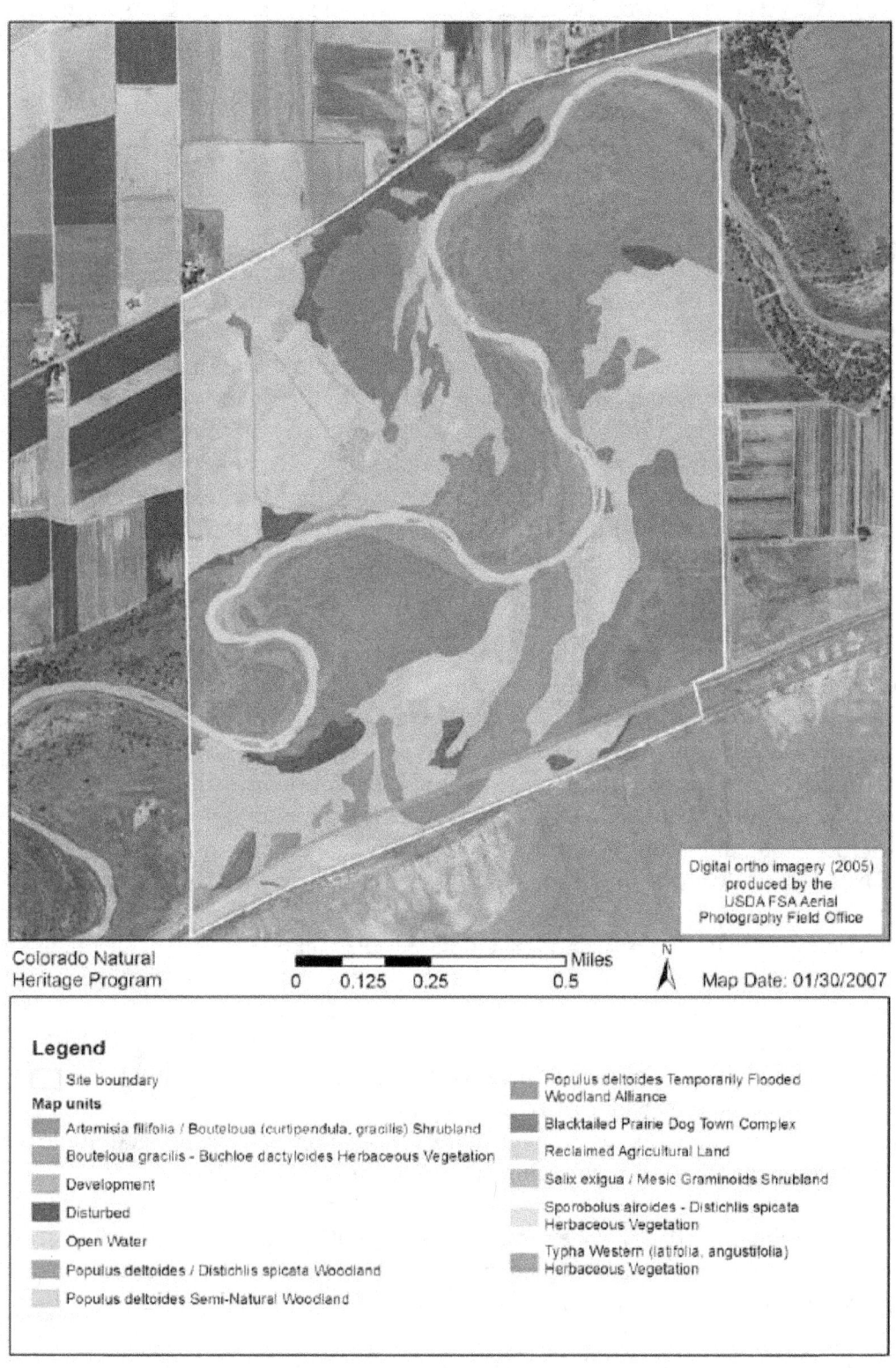

Figure 7. Vegetation map for Bent's Old Fort NHS (from Stevens *et al.* 2007).

23

spicata) and alkali sacaton (*Sporobolus airoides*). In some areas, the cottonwoods are sparse and grade into grassy meadows. Along the terraces, the vegetation transitions to shortgrass prairie. The habitat along the Arkansas River at the NHS contains large occurrences of globally rare plains cottonwood ecosystems (www.cnhp.colostate.edu/.../L4_PCA-Arkansas%20River%20at%20Bent's%20Fort_7-23-2010.pdf). These cottonwood communities are known only from the lower Arkansas and Cimarron river watersheds in Colorado, Kansas and Oklahoma.

River Geomorphology

The current Arkansas River in the area of the NHS is an alluvial, sand-bottomed, broadly meandering, perennial river. The average gradient is approximately 6.7 ft/mile. Over a linear distance of 3 miles, the river meanders nearly 6 miles. The river's meanders are developed on a floodplain that to the north of the river is approximately 1 mile in width, very flat and bordered by low bluffs or hills. The floodplain to the south is 0.25 to 0.5 miles wide. Overall, the floodplain is developed in unconsolidated materials underlain by 30 to 40 feet of sediment. The sediment load is moderately heavy – largely of silt and sand. The river has been aggrading for the past several decades in the area between La Junta and John Martin Dam (30 miles downstream) (Watts and Lindner-Lunsford 1992; Gates *et al.* 2006) . The natural flow regime of the Arkansas River was altered by the construction of the Pueblo Dam and Reservoir (approximately 60 miles upstream) in 1965.

As the hydrology of the river changed from intermittent to perennial with the advent of irrigation (Nadler and Schumm 1981), the floodplain saw a concomitant change in the types and amount of vegetation. Historically woody vegetation was sparse along the river (Swenson 1970, Nadler and Schumm 1981). Floodplain vegetation is much denser today because higher soil moisture is sustained from a higher water table associated with perennial flow. Additionally, the introduction of exotic salt cedar (*Tamarix ramosissima*), a phreatophyte, disrupted the vegetative dynamics of the floodplain. Significant morphological changes were wrought along the Arkansas River because of these hydrologic and vegetative changes. Droughts, coupled with a decrease in sediment supply due to irrigation diversion and the construction of dams also affected the channels. All of these factors acted to stabilize an otherwise active channel morphology.

Because of these changes, Nadler and Schumm (1981) described the Arkansas River in eastern Colorado as a river that has undergone a metamorphosis. Schumm (1969) defined river metamorphosis as a complete change of river morphology, for example, from meandering to braided and vice versa. The Arkansas River in the 19th century was wide, shallow and braided; the river today is defined by different channel characteristics (Table 2).

Figure 8 depicts the manner of river metamorphosis at Bent's Old Fort National Historic Site. Point-bar stabilization and meander-loop enlargement are primary characteristics of this hypothesis. Nadler and Schumm (1981) describe the metamorphosis as follows:

> Perennial flows, droughts and especially dense salt-cedar growth were major factors leading to the metamorphosis. Salt cedar colonized the channel below mean high water level and stabilized the point bars during the drought of the 1930s. This process allowed meander loops to enlarge as channel width decreased. At elevation A [Figure 8] the

alluvium becomes coarser-grained toward the channel as expected; whereas, at elevation C it becomes finer-grained from right to left. The change to finer-grained sediment is the result of a change in the type of sediment transported through the reach. This change is the result of the incision of Timpas Creek, a deeply incised channel that introduced a large suspended load into the Arkansas River.

The NHS was recently (2004) successful in the eradication of salt cedar from within its boundaries. It remains to be seen how the removal of salt cedar manifests into changes, if any, in river channel morphology and the magnitude of those changes.

Nadler and Schumm (1981) noted that the change from intermittent to perennial flow in the Arkansas River and the resulting shift from a braided to meandering channel was analogous to a change in climate. Usually, changes in flood peaks or mean annual discharge explain river response, but in the case of the Arkansas River at the NHS, a change in discharge frequency resulted in major channel adjustments.

Table 2. Changes in fluvial geomorphologic features of the Arkansas River at Bent's Old Fort National Historic Site, 1870-1977 (adapted from Nadler and Schumm 1981). See Nadler and Schumm (1981) for variable definitions.

Variable	1870	1892	1926	1952	1977
% silt-clay					5.01
Median grain size (mm/Φ)			1.27/-0.344		0.248/2.010
Sediment sorting (Φ)			2.301		0.618
Vegetation	Large cottonwoods, little underbrush, no salt cedars		Salt cedars, cottonwoods, willows		
Valley slope		.0016		.0018	
Channel slope	.0013	.0014	.0015	.0010	
Sinuosity	1.20	1.10	1.21	1.84	1.89
Width (m)	185	225	225	45	30
Width/depth ratio	Greater than 17				17
Floodplain construction	Point bar formation				
Channel change	Braided to meandering channel				

MWH (2005) recently classified segments of the lower Arkansas River based on the geomorphic characterization of Rosgen (1996). Rosgen's classification is based on four hierarchical levels; MWH used only Levels I and II to describe the morphology of the lower Arkansas River. Level I classifies stream segments based on channel slope, channel shape, and channel patterns. The Level II classification considers factors such as entrenchment ratio, width/depth ratio, sinuosity, channel slope, and channel materials. The last segment classified by MWH (2005) ended at La Junta – it is the opinion of the authors that the segment of the river that includes the NHS would be classified the same as that of the segment ending at La Junta. That classification would be, in Rosgen's terminology, a C5c stream segment. This represents a single-threaded channel that is slightly entrenched, has a moderate width/depth ratio and a moderate sinuosity, with a slope that is <0.001, and a sand substrate. Such a classification means that the current Arkansas River of the NHS would have a very high sensitivity to disturbance with a fair recovery potential. In addition, it would also have a very high potential for stream bank erosion, very high sediment supply, and a very high potential for vegetation to control the width/depth ratio (MHW 2005). The Rosgen stream geomorphic classification represents a formalized, index-based approach that incorporates the basic variables described by Nadler and Schumm (1981). It allows one to typecast a river segment for how that segment may respond to various restoration techniques.

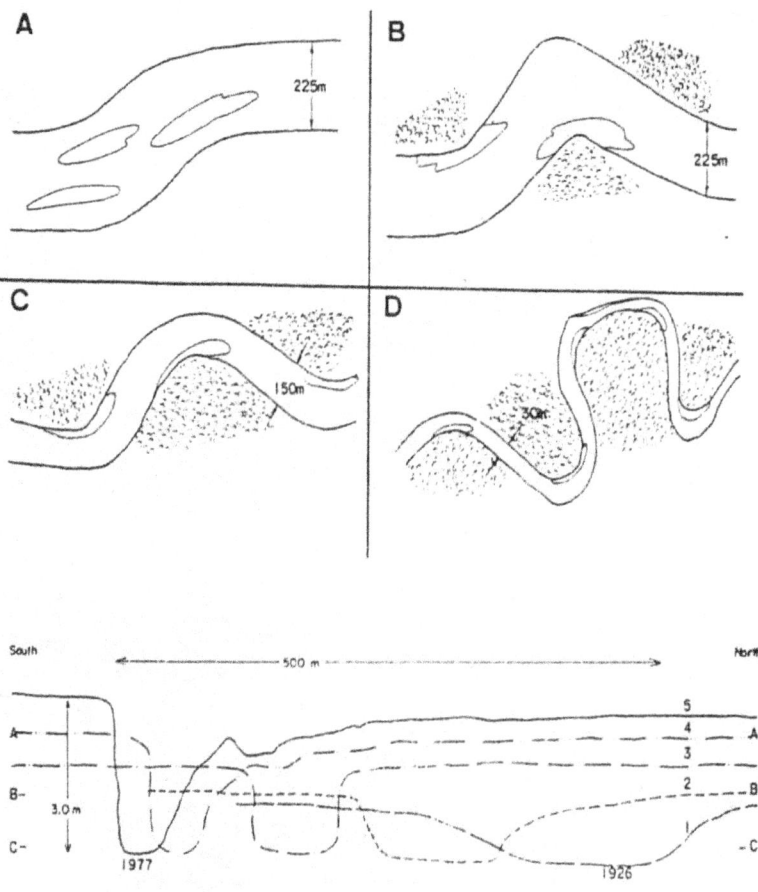

Figure 8. Hypothesized metamorphosis in the Arkansas River at Bent's Old Fort National Historic Site (taken from Figures 12 and 13 in Nadler and Schumm 1981). <u>Upper</u>: A – pre-1900 channel; B – 1926 channel; C– channel between 1926 and 1953; D – modern channel. <u>Lower</u>: cross-sectional changes. Line 1 – 1926 channel location; Lines 2, 3 and 4 – transitional channel locations; Line 5 – 1977 channel location.

Hydrogeology

The primary aquifer along the lower Arkansas River of Colorado is the alluvial aquifer (http://www.geosurvey.state.co.us/wateratlas). With depths up to 250 ft, this Quaternary age alluvium extends along the Arkansas River for 150 miles from Pueblo, CO to the Kansas state line (MWH 2005). The alluvial aquifer consists of unconsolidated river-deposited sediments (a heterogeneous mix of sands, gravels, silts, and clays). It is an unconfined, water-table aquifer in direct hydraulic connection with the Arkansas River surface water, and is underlain by relatively impermeable Cretaceous bedrock. Water table depth ranges from approximately 5 to 30 ft below ground surface along much of the lower river. Over 3,400 wells have been installed in the lower Arkansas River alluvium, and over 90 percent of these wells are completed at depths less than 120 ft below ground surface with an average depth of only 58 ft (http://www.geosurvey.state.co.us/wateratlas). General basin wide hydraulic characteristics for the lower Arkansas River alluvium include: transmissivity of 2,000-60,000 ft^2/day; hydraulic conductivity of 70-1,200 ft/day with an average of 530 ft/day; discharge of 10-4,000 gallons per minute (gpm) with a mean of 360 gpm; specific capacity of 7-54 gpm/ft drawdown; and specific yield of 0.13-0.20 (http://www.geosurvey.state.co.us/wateratlas).

In most areas, water table depth in the alluvial aquifer is affected by proximity to the Arkansas River or variability in agricultural use (approximately 2 million acre-feet of river water were diverted for irrigation in 1998). From 1971 to 2000, wells closer to the river had a higher, less variable water table (MWH 2005). For that time period in Otero and Crowley counties, water table depth for wells close to the Arkansas River ranged from 6 to 25 ft below ground surface and for wells farther from the river from 21 to 44 ft below ground surface (MHW 2005). Greater than average precipitation from 1982-1999 is a potential cause of increased water table elevation during this period (USGS 2002). Ground water withdrawals are lower during wet years and infiltration is higher, resulting in a higher water table (MHW 2005).

Weist *et al.* (1965) found that the alluvial aquifer near the NHS consists of Holocene and Pleistocene alluvial deposits. This aquifer is relatively shallow, unconfined, and highly transmissive (Watts and Lindner-Lunsford 1992); the ground water gradient (easterly direction) is approximately 6 ft/mi in the La Junta area (MHC 2005). Because the Arkansas River partially penetrates the aquifer, it acts as both a source of recharge or discharge to the aquifer (Watts and Lindner-Lunsford 1992, NPS 2005). Recharge to the aquifer is through leakage from the Arkansas River (e.g., short-term increases in river stage lead to short-term increases in water table elevation in wells near the river) and Fort Lyon Canal (leakage increases with increasing stage), deep percolation of irrigation water and precipitation, and underflow. The Fort Lyon Canal is unlined and has a direct relation to ground water levels. Bossong (2000) reported conveyance losses for the canal of up to 15 ac-ft/day/canal mile. The Fryingpan-Arkansas Project and other water development projects that import water to the basin have increased stream flow in the lower Arkansas River, further enhancing recharge (MWH 2005).

Discharges from the aquifer include leakage to the Arkansas River, pumpage for municipal, irrigation and industrial supplies, evapotranspiration, and underflow. The long-term mean for ground water withdrawals from 1972-1994 in the La Junta area was 1.64 ft/yr for municipal and irrigation use (Bossong 2000). Additionally important is the aggradation of the Arkansas River bed, which increases river stage and temporarily increases leakage from the river to the aquifer

(NPS 2005). During high river flows, a local reversal of the hydraulic gradient between the alluvial aquifer and the Arkansas River can occur (NPS 2005). Watts and Lindner-Lunsford (1992) and Bossong (2000) noted the fluctuation of the water table over the last three decades of the 20th century -- the decline of water levels in the 1970s corresponded with a period of reduced flow in the Fort Lyon Canal (see Figure 15 and associated discussion) while water level increases of the 1980s correlated with increased flow in the Canal, increased surface water applications, and reduced ground water withdrawals (Bossong 2000). As mentioned above, an increase in precipitation over the long-term mean may be a proximate cause for the water table increase in the 1980s.

Woods *et al*. (2002) conducted a short-term study (March-September 2001) into the cause of basement flooding at Bent's Old Fort. The cause of this flooding had been attributed to rising water table levels in the late 1990s and early 2000s (Bossong 2000). The purpose of the study was to determine which of several factors (i.e., decline in groundwater pumping; increased seepage from Fort Lyon Canal; increased deep percolation of irrigation water; and greater leakage from Arkansas River to the aquifer due to river bed aggradation) was primarily responsible for causing flooding of the Fort's basement. They installed a network of 15 wells to monitor ground water elevation. Upland wells had relatively stable water elevations and were unresponsive to river stage changes; however, wells closest to the Arkansas River were more variable and distinctly responsive to river stage changes. Furthermore, the reach of the Arkansas River in the NHS was a gaining reach – the ground water gradient was towards the river because water table levels were higher than the river stage. Thus, river stage was less of an influence on water table levels along this river reach than in the area near La Junta (Bossong 2000).

Ground Water Quality
All ground water at the NHS is classed as sodium-calcium-sulfate-bicarbonate in character (NPS 2005) and is rated hard to very hard (Weist *et al*. 1965).

The Colorado Department of Public Health and the Environment (2006) determined that ground water in the alluvial aquifer of the lower Arkansas River basin meets primary and secondary federal and state domestic or municipal water supply standards, based on a detailed analysis of wells of the aquifer. Only 1 out of 20 wells had nitrate concentrations that exceeded the water quality standard of 10 mg/L. Detections of herbicides and pesticides were low and all detections of pesticides were at concentrations below the water quality standard and health advisory levels. Similar to surface water, the alluvial ground water frequently exceeds the high salinity hazard threshold for agriculture of 50 μS/cm and the 500 mg/L drinking water secondary maximum concentration level (CDPHE 2002).

From 1999-2005 Gates *et al*. (2006) studied salinity as a function of specific conductance concentrations in the ground water (from approximately 90 wells) of a large study area that included the NHS. Mean specific conductance was 3,275 μS/cm, well above the agriculturally-based very high salinity hazard of 2,250 μS/cm, and demonstrated high spatial variability over the range of wells sample (Figure 9). Irrigation frequency and geology are two of several factors that could cause this variability (Gates *et al*. 2006).

Ground water salinity has increased in the Arkansas River alluvial aquifer since the 1970s (Gates *et al*. 2006). Gates *et al*. listed the following as possible reasons: 1) reduced ground water pumping; 2) gains in seepage losses from irrigation canals; 3) failures of tile drains installed in the 1930s; 4) changes in river operations,; and 4) dissolution of salts from salt-bearing geologic formations that form the base underneath the alluvial aquifer.

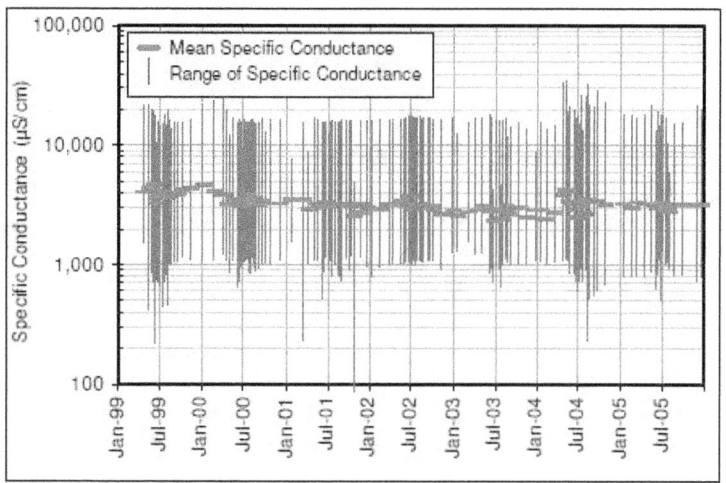

Figure 9. Mean and spatial variation of specific conductance in the lower Arkansas River alluvial ground water (from MWH 2008). Based on samples from 90 wells.

Gates *et al*. (2006) found that ground water concentrations of selenium averaged approximately 57.7 μg/L. For comparison, the state chronic standard for aquatic habitat of surface waters is 4.5 μg/L. They found that regional geologic formations had a strong influence on ground water selenium concentrations. There was an inverse correlation between selenium concentration and distance to the closest upstream shale, and selenium concentrations from samples taken from shale-derived material had a median concentration of 30.8 μg/L; whereas alluvial material had a median concentration of 12.2 μg/L. Additionally, they demonstrated a strong correlation between dissolved selenium and both total dissolved solids and uranium in ground water.

Aquifers overlying or adjacent to Cretaceous age marine shales and sedimentary rock formations typically have higher ground water concentrations of salinity, iron, and selenium (Seiler *et al*. 1999, Burkhalter and Gates 2005). Figure 10 shows the location and extent of Cretaceous marine shales in the Arkansas River Basin. The Pierre Shale is known to be seleniferous.

The lines of evidence for other Cretaceous marine shales (*e.g*., Carlile and Graneros shales and Greenhorn limestone) being seleniferous is indirect (Seiler *et al*. 1999). For example, there are ground water hotspots throughout the Arkansas River basin. Evaporative concentration of selenium would result in more uniform concentrations basin-wide, thus it appears that these selenium hotspots are geologically derived (Donnelly and Gates 2005).

Surface Water Hydrology
The Arkansas River basin is the largest basin in Colorado (Figure 11), covering 28,286 mi^2 (> 18 million acres), yet only 20 percent of the state's population occupies this area. The river originates in the mountains near Leadville and continues to the state line in Kansas, with an approximate flow of 1 million ac-ft/yr. Major tributaries include the Purgatoire, Huerfano,

Cucharas, and Apishipa rivers. The basin is usually characterized as two subsections, the upper and lower Arkansas River.

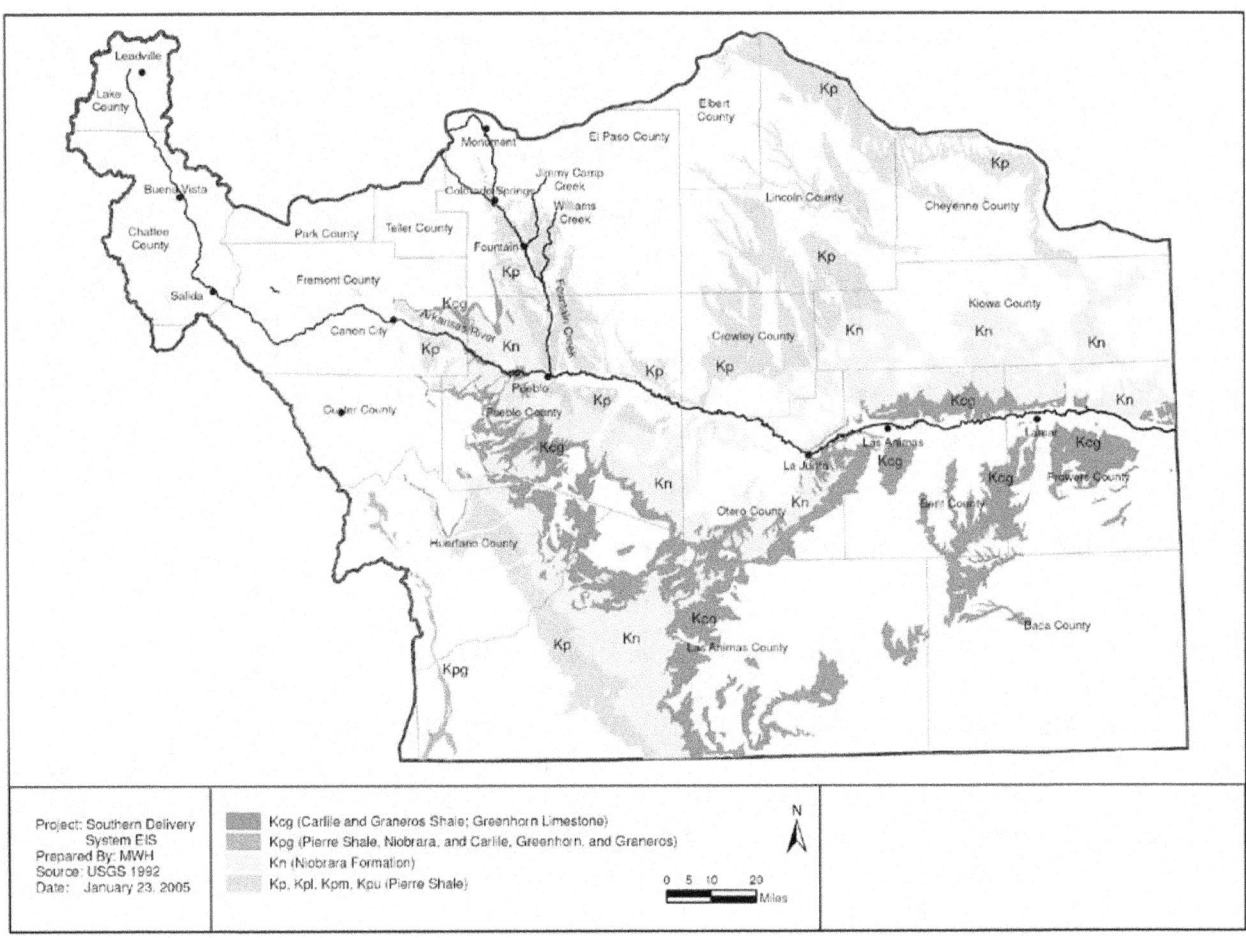

Figure 10. Locations of Cretaceous marine shale in the Arkansas River Basin of Colorado (from MWH 2008).

The upper Arkansas River of Colorado is generally considered to be from the mountain source to Pueblo Dam, while the lower section continues from the Pueblo Dam to the Kansas state line. The upper Arkansas contains mountain streams and tributaries and often runs colder and quicker due to fewer diversions; it is utilized mainly for municipal drinking water supplies. The lower Arkansas River of Colorado is a wider, shallower flowing river heavily diverted in canals and reservoirs for agricultural and municipal purposes. Canals contribute largely to the hydrologic regime with diversions re-routing about 2 million ac-ft/yr of water for irrigation in the lower Arkansas River basin of Colorado.

The NHS is in the Upper Arkansas Lake Meredith watershed (HUC 1102000, as defined by the U.S. Geological Survey; Figure 12). In this case 'Upper Arkansas' refers to the upper part of the overall Arkansas River watershed. Within this watershed there are approximately 1,413,670 acres of land utilized for farming or ranching. The population of this watershed is slightly greater than 100,000.

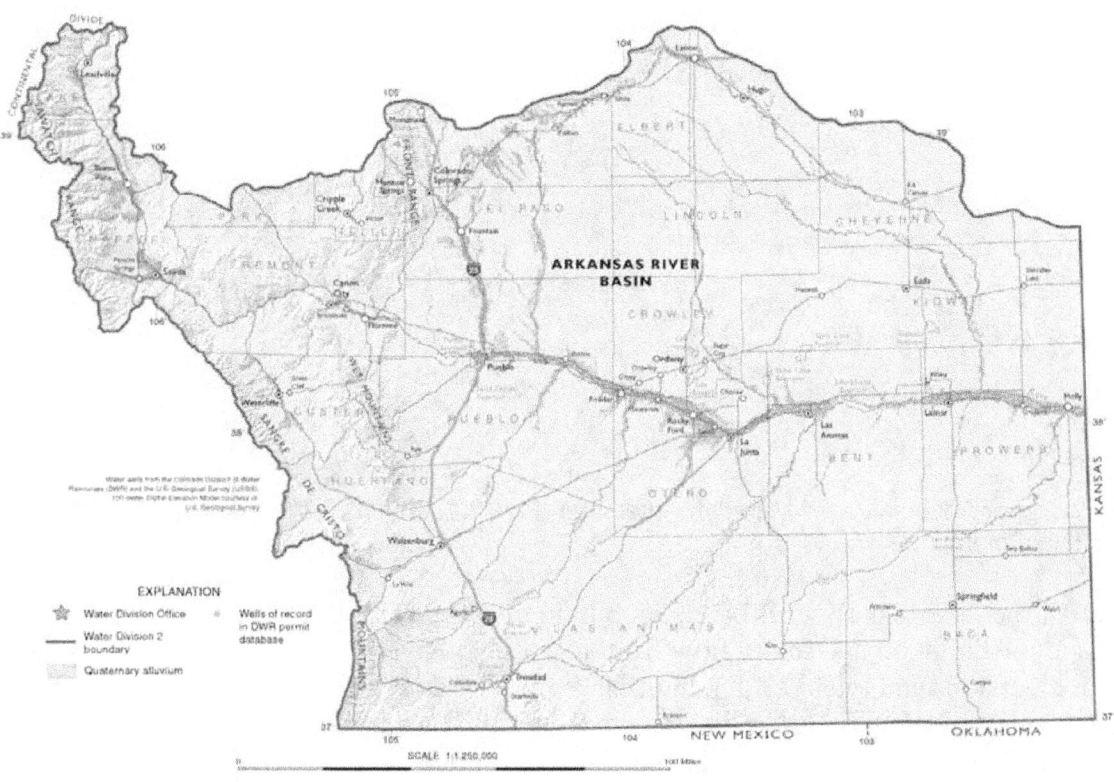

Figure 11. The Arkansas River basin in Colorado (from Tetra Tech 2007).

Drainage problems usually appear in intensively-irrigated alluvial valleys within a few decades to a few hundred years of the commencement of large-scale irrigation. Eventually, the artificially high rate of application of water to land exceeds the natural rate of drainage, the water table rises, and artificial drainage is needed to regain an acceptable water and salt balance (Gates and Grismer 1989). In the lower Arkansas River valley in Colorado, saline high water tables began to appear in the early part of the 20th century. Installations of subsurface drains in the 1930s seemed to alleviate the problems; however, water tables began to rise again in the 1970s. Watts and Lindner-Lundsford (1992) suggested that the blame be placed on increased diversions from the river for irrigation application and associated reduction in ground water pumping. In the 1950s-1970s two reservoirs began operations that have drastically changed the river. Flushing from floods was substantially reduced and controlled releases were made from the reservoirs. This allowed year-round or at least prolonged supplies of water to the canals on the perimeter of the valley. Seepage from these canals and lower velocity in the river has caused sediments to deposit on the bed and the river level to rise. Recent investigations at Colorado State University of water levels in the reach of the Arkansas River upstream of John Martin Reservoir indicate an increasing trend since about 1989. The overall rise in the river level (of about 0.6 m) may have significantly reduced the gradient that drives drainage flows from the irrigated land to the river. Also, in response to the recent Kansas –Colorado court ruling, ground water pumping in the valley which serves to reduce water table levels has diminished.

31

Figure 12. Upper Arkansas Lake Meredith watershed (HUC 11020005) in the Arkansas River basin of southeastern Colorado.

The flow of the Arkansas River is perennial but highly regulated; the flow of its tributaries depends on precipitation and return flow from irrigation. River flow is affected by numerous upstream diversions and Pueblo Dam, built in 1965. The dam lies approximately 62 miles upstream from the NHS. For example, stream flow at Las Animas is substantially smaller than at the upstream sites. The downstream decrease in stream flow is attributable to irrigation diversions upstream of Las Animas (Lewis 1998).

Using historical (1974-2004) instantaneous peak discharge data, MWH (2005) summarized peak flows for the Arkansas River at the La Junta gage site (USGS gage 07102300) as follows:

Peak Flow Discharge (cfs)					
1.5-year	**2-year**	**10-year**	**50-year**	**100-year**	**500-year**
2,700	4,200	14,200	29,600	38,300	64,800

The maximum recorded instantaneous peak discharge for the La Junta gage was recorded on June 4, 1921 at 200,000 cfs (MWH 2005).

The Arkansas River is dominated by the seasonal snowmelt cycle; baseline flow conditions exist September-April followed by an increase in flow in May to a peak in June and gradually tapering flows until base conditions are reached in September (Figure 13). Prior to European settlement the Arkansas River had strongly varying, intermittent flow during each year (Figure 14), with very little discharge during the dry times of the year and large floods in late spring and summer. Following settlement of the plains, land-use practices so altered the water and sediment flows along the Arkansas River that the channel underwent a change in channel functioning and pattern (see *River Geomorphology* section). The primary influence was flow regulation (Pueblo and John Martin dams) and diversion (e.g., Fort Lyon Canal, Figures 15 and 16), which reduced seasonal flood peaks (Figure 14, post-1965) and increased dry-season base flow in the channels. For example, base flows during December-April for the period 1970-1999 increased from 1.3 to 2+ times more that the base flows from 1912-1938 (based on data collected from La Junta stream gage). As irrigation water that was diverted and spread across agricultural fields filtered into the subsurface, regional water tables rose (see *Hydrogeology* section). The amount of sediment carried by the Arkansas River decreased as the reservoirs behind Pueblo and John Martin dams served as large settling tanks, and the smaller seasonal high flows had less energy to carry sediment.

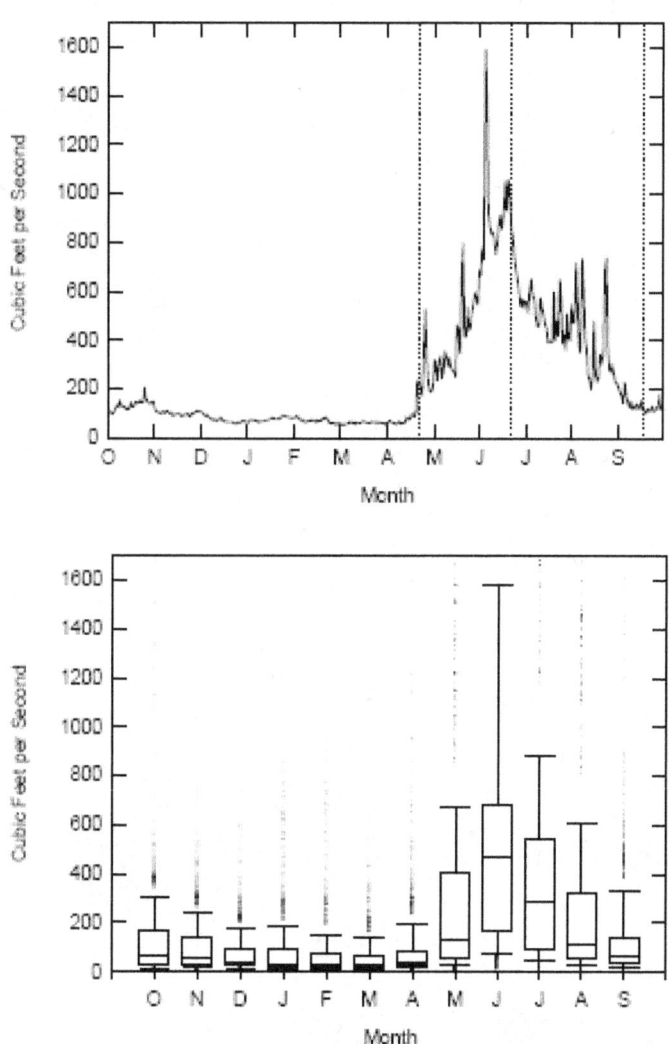

Representative mean annual hydrograph (top) and distribution of daily flows by month (bottom) for hydrologic season determination. Box and whiskers represent a five number summary; bottom whisker cap is 10th percentile, bottom of box is 25th percentile, internal line is median, top of box is 75th percentile, and top whisker is 90th percentile. Hydrologic seasons for Bent's Old Fort National Historic Site are: Sep. 15 to Apr. 19, Apr. 20 to Jun. 19, and Jun. 20 to Sep. 14.

Figure 13. Representative hydrographs for the Arkansas River at La Junta, CO (USGS gage station 07123000) (from NPS 1998).

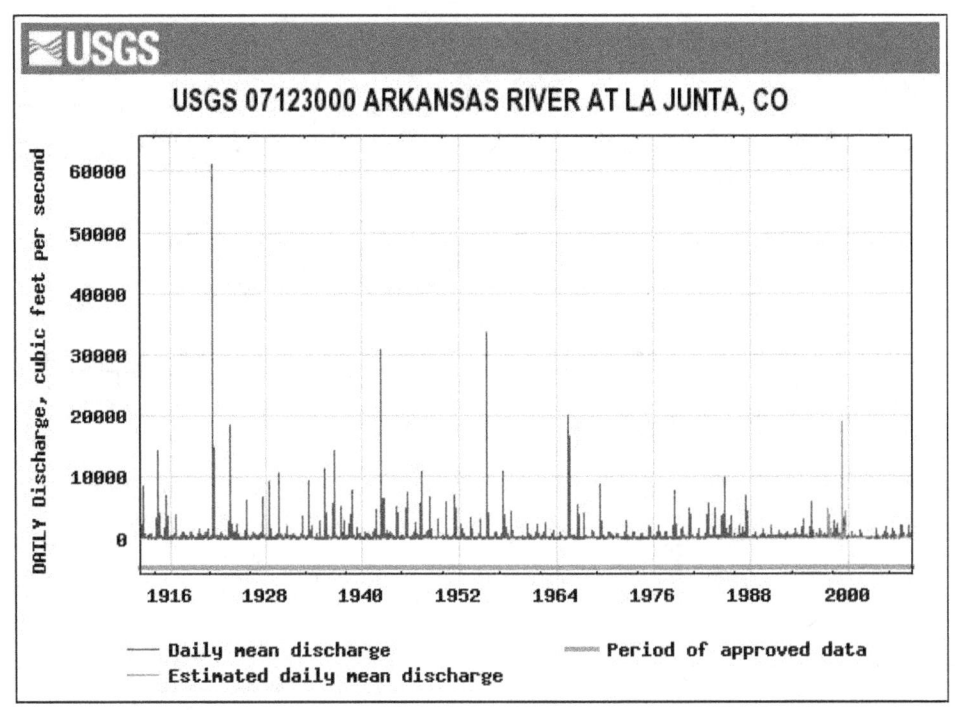

Figure 14. Mean daily discharge from 1912-2007 for the Arkansas River at La Junta, CO. Pre-1960 flows are the closest representation of flow variability prior to European settlement. Compare the variability of flows pre-1965 to post-1965, the completion date for Pueblo Dam and Reservoir (from http://waterdata.usgs.gov/co/nwis/inventory/?site_no=07123000).

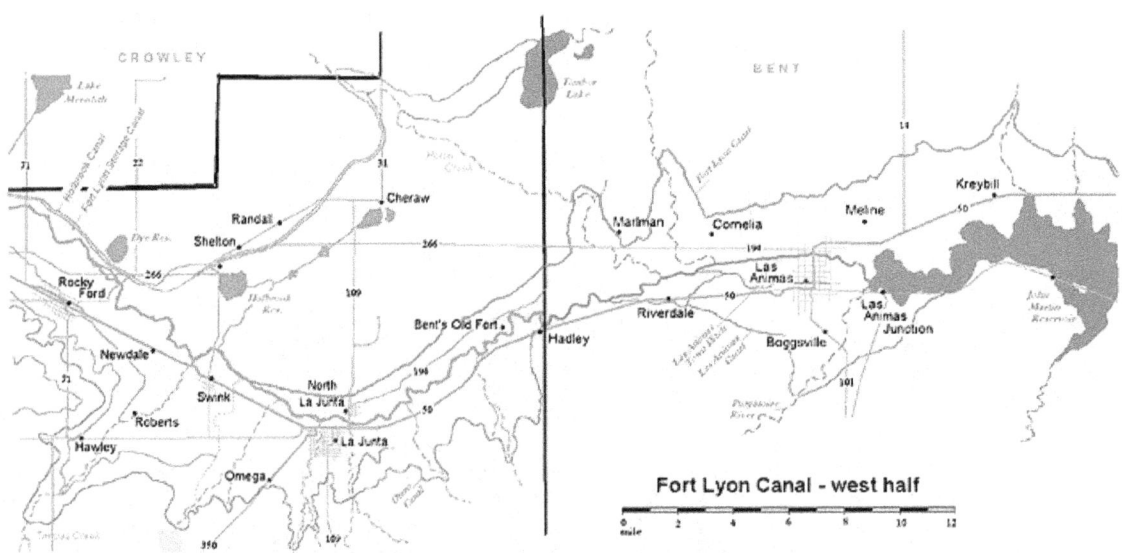

Figure 15. Map of Lower Arkansas River from Rocky Ford to John Martin Reservoir showing location of the Fort Lyon Canal (red) in relation to the river and Bent's Old Fort NHS. The canal was developed in 1886 by T.C. Henry. In the vicinity of the NHS it lies approximately ½ mile to the north. It is an earthen canal supplying irrigation water to farms in the lower Arkansas Valley. This earthen canal is currently use to supply water for agricultural irrigation and is managed by the Fort Lyon Canal Co.

34

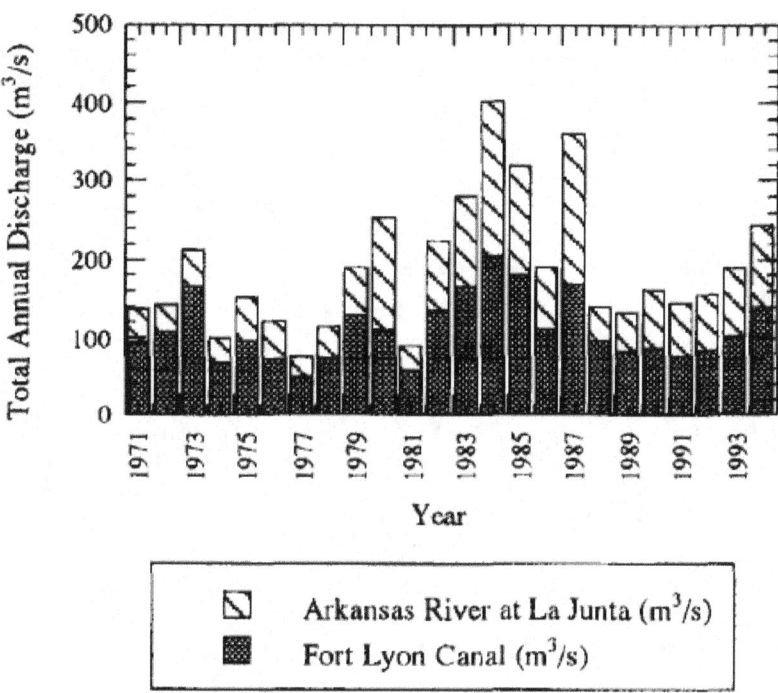

Figure 16. Total annual discharge of the Arkansas River at La Junta and Fort Lyon Canal,1917-1994, showing the disparity in flow between the two systems (from Goff *et al*. 1998).

A limited glimpse (1974-2006) of mean annual flows for the Arkansas River (Figure 17) suggests that the drought cycle in the southeastern Colorado has a recurrence interval of approximately 11 to 13 years.

Besides the Arkansas River, the NHS has a few small irrigation ditches, remnants of past agricultural use,, that are not presently used by the NHS. An active irrigation return ditch flows eastward along State Route 194 and empties into the Arkansas River just north of the Arch Wetland (see Figure 24).

Existing stream staff gages along the Arkansas River inside NHS boundaries (from the study by Woods *et al*. 2002) are not currently monitored by NHS staff., because they are consistently damaged by flood waters. The NHS should seek technical assistance from the Water Resources Division to explore the durability issue of these gages.

Surface Water Quality
The following history and description of the Arkansas River provides the necessary context for understanding water quality in the river. It is taken from http://www.kgs.ku.edu/Hydro/UARC/background.html and has been slightly modified for this report.

> Before settlement of the Great Plains in the 1800's, Arkansas River flows carried dissolved solids primarily derived from Cretaceous bedrock in southeastern Colorado and southwestern Kansas near the state line. The dissolved solids inputs entered the river from tributaries and ground-water discharge. During low and moderate flows, the river waters were probably slightly saline as they entered Kansas. As the flows passed through

southeast Colorado, they could either recharge to or receive discharge from the alluvial aquifer, depending on the amount of flow and the ground-water levels in the aquifer.

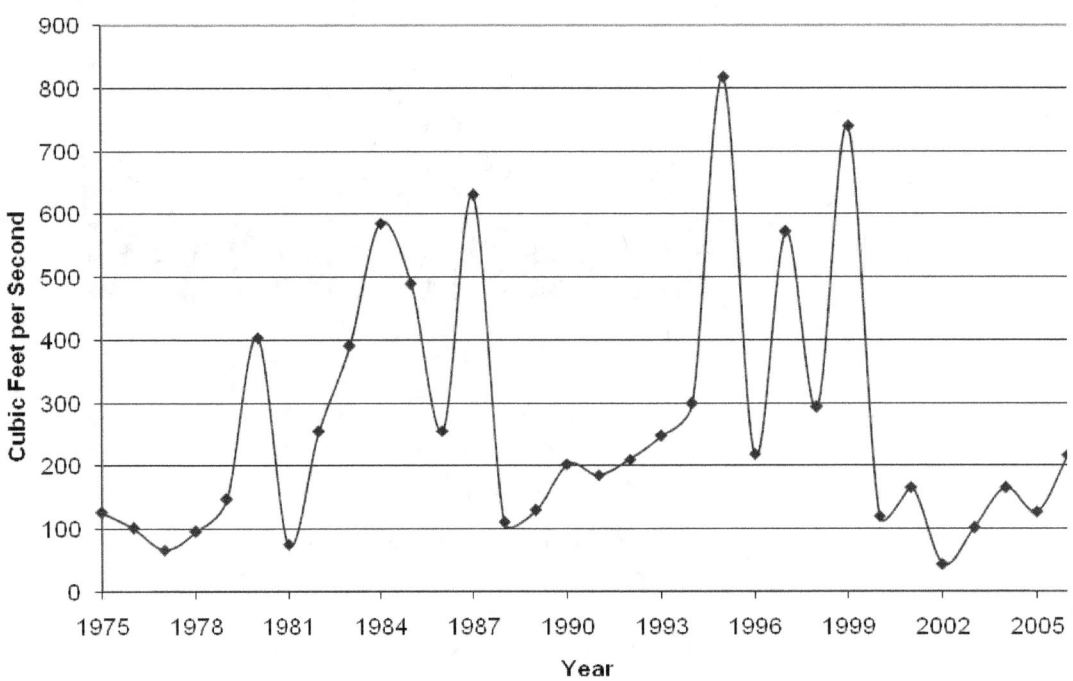

Figure 17. Mean annual flow (cfs) from 1975-2006 for the Las Animas, CO gage site (USGS 07124000) on the Arkansas River.

High-flow conditions following dry periods would be times of greater recharge. However, during flood conditions, the Arkansas River waters were more dilute and could have recharged the alluvial aquifer with fresher waters. The bank storage would then have been returned to the river as discharge in later dry periods after partially mixing with waters in the alluvium.

Beginning in the 1860's, farmers dug small ditches along the Arkansas River in Colorado to divert water for crop irrigation. Larger canals were then constructed for extensive diversion systems starting in the 1870's in Colorado. Evapotranspiration of the diverted waters increased the salinity of ground-water recharge from the fields and irrigation return flows. Part of the dissolved solids in ground waters underlying diversion ditches and the fields irrigated by the ditch waters was attributed to concentrated river waters. Ground-water levels rose in the vicinity of the canals and ditches due to leakage.

Irrigation from diversions of Arkansas River water in southeastern Colorado has increased the salinity of river water since the 1870's due to evapotranspiration concentration. Regulation of river flows by the John Martin Reservoir beginning about 1950 further increased the salinity problem through increased diversions and consumptive loss by evapotranspiration in southeastern Colorado. The evapotranspiration caused increases in many dissolved constituents to undesirable levels for water use.

The NPS (1998) provided a baseline water quality data inventory and retrospective analysis for the NHS. Water quality data were retrieved from national databases (e.g., STORET) for the NHS and its surrounding area. The results for the study area yielded 11,722 observations for 149 separate parameters collected by the NPS, USGS, USEPA, and CDPHE at 30 monitoring stations from 1901 through 1995. Approximately 54 percent of the 11,722 observations within the study area were collected by the CDPHE from 1901 through 1993 in the Arkansas River at the Fort Lyon Canal. However, no stations were located within the NHS boundary, and the three Arkansas River sites are all over 5 miles upstream near La Junta. Many of the monitoring stations represent either one-time or intensive single-year sampling efforts by the collecting agencies. Only five stations (three mainstem and two tributary) within the study area yielded longer-term records consisting of multiple observations for several important water quality parameters. The results of the NHS water quality criteria screen found 18 groups of parameters that exceeded screening criteria at least once within the study area. Dissolved oxygen, pH, chloride, chlorine, cadmium, copper, lead, nickel, selenium, and zinc exceeded their respective U.S. Environmental Protection Agency criteria for protection of freshwater aquatic life. Chloride, fluoride, sulfate, nitrite plus nitrate, cadmium, chromium, lead, nickel, uranium and zinc exceeded their respective U.S. Environmental Protection Agency drinking water criteria. Fecal-indicator bacteria concentrations (total coliform and fecal coliform) and turbidity exceeded the NPS-Water Resources Division screening limits for freshwater bathing and aquatic life.

The NHS is in Segment COARLA01b of the Arkansas River as delineated by the CDPHE. This segment is classified according to the following uses: 1) Aquatic Life – Class 2 (waters that are not capable of sustaining a wide variety of warm water biota, due to physical habitat, water flows or levels, or uncorrectable water quality conditions that result in substantial impairment of the abundance and diversity of species); 2) Recreation – Class E (use for primary contact recreation or has been used for such activities since November 28, 1975); 3) Domestic Water Supply (waters are suitable for potable water supplies—after receiving standard treatment these waters will meet Colorado drinking water regulations); and 4) Agriculture (suitable for irrigation of crops usually grown in Colorado and not hazardous as drinking water for livestock). Additionally, Segment COARLA01b is a use-protected water under Colorado's antidegradation designations. This means that this segment does not warrant protection provided by the outstanding waters designation or the antidegradation review process. Use protection provides the lowest protection of the three Colorado antidegradation designations.

Numeric water quality standards are assigned to water bodies to protect classified uses. Numeric standards can either apply on a statewide basis or to specific waters. General water quality standards, known as Table Value Standards (TVS) are assigned for the Arkansas River Basin in Regulation #42 (CDPHE 2007). Site-specific standards for segments are also assigned which may or may not be equal to the TVS. The water quality standards, including TVS and site specific standards for the Arkansas River basin are summarized at
http://www.cdphe.state.co.us/regulations/wqccregs/ .

The State of Colorado published in 2008 Colorado's List of Water-Quality-Limited Segments Requiring Total Maximum Daily Loads (TMDLs), commonly referred to as the 303(d) list. This list was prepared to fulfill section 303(d) of the Clean Water Act that requires states submit to the U.S. Environmental Protection Agency a list of those waters for which technology-based effluent limitations and other required controls are not stringent enough to implement water quality standards. Once listed, the State is required to prioritize these segments based on the severity of pollution and other factors. It will then determine the cause(s) of the water quality problem and allocate the responsibility for controlling the pollution. This analysis is called the TMDL process, and it is a pollution reduction plan that identifies the maximum amount of a pollutant a water body can receive without violating water quality standards. The TMDL process identifies both point and nonpoint sources of each pollutant and determines how much each source must reduce its contribution in order to meet the standard. The total of all contributions must be less than the maximum daily load. Subsequent to the TMDL, a detailed implementation plan is developed that focuses on source reduction strategies to meet water quality standards. The 2008 Colorado 303(d) list showed that segment COARLA01b as water quality limited for selenium. The development of a TMDL for this segment was also listed as a low priority. Previously, this segment was on the 303 (d) list for fecal coliform; however, a fecal coliform-based TMDL was completed in 1998 (NPS 2003).

Selenium is a naturally occurring semi-metallic trace element that is essential for animals in small doses but is toxic at high concentrations. Selenium has had adverse effects on endangered fish species in the Gunnison and Colorado rivers in Colorado; however, in the lower Arkansas River basin, there was no evidence of impacts to aquatic biota (Mueller *et al*. 1991), although some segments not only exceed selenium water quality standards, they are at levels exceeding 10 ppb known to eliminate fish in some parts of the country. Possible explanations for these site-specific differences in toxicity of selenium include:

- Different forms of selenium have different effects on aquatic life. The dominant form of selenium in water can vary based on site-specific factors (Maier *et al*. 1987). The dominant toxic form of selenium is selenite – selenite represents a small percentage of the selenium in the lower Arkansas River (USEPA 1998);
- Sulfate concentrations in the lower Arkansas River increase downstream of Pueblo (Figure 18) and may reduce selenium toxicity [see Brix *et al*. (2001) for a discussion of the sulfate/selenium toxicity relationship];
- Aquatic life in the Arkansas River Basin may have adapted to survive in waters with elevated selenium concentrations.

There has been considerable uncertainty regarding the appropriate selenium standards for different stream segments in the Arkansas River basin. The current TVS for acute and chronic dissolved selenium are 18.4 and 4.6 μg/L, respectively. The average selenium concentration in the Arkansas River Segment COARLA01b is 15.66 μg/L (Tetra Tech 2007). Figure 19 shows average selenium concentrations for specific locations on the Lower Arkansas River and its major tributaries.

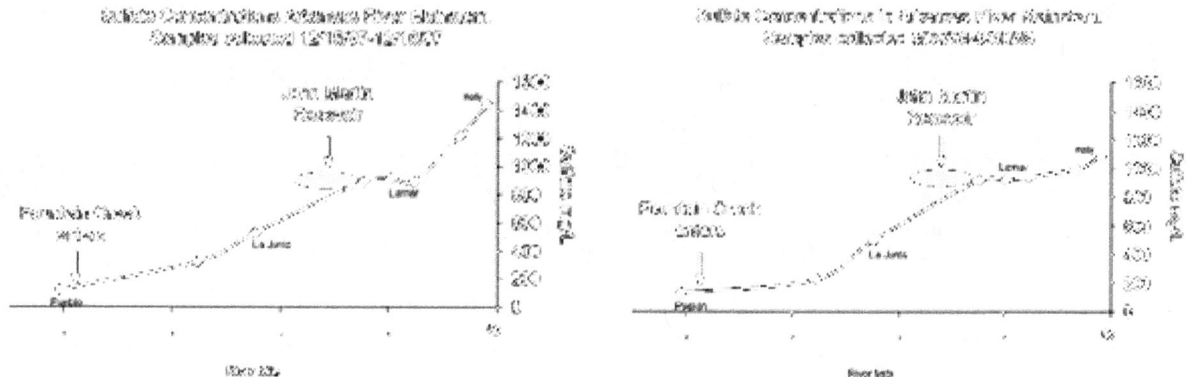

Figure 18. Sulfate concentrations along the lower Arkansas River in Colorado (From http://ndis1.nrel.colostate.edu/waterquality/arkrnut/arknut.html.

Ortiz *et al.* (1998) found that over 90 percent of the selenium measured in the lower Arkansas River was in the dissolved phase. In general, selenium concentrations increased downstream from Pueblo Reservoir to Las Animas. Salinity in the lower Arkansas River has the same spatial pattern. Some of the factors causing an increase in salinity in the lower Arkansas River may also be responsible for increasing selenium in the downstream direction. Donnelly and Gates (1995) investigated relationships between water quality parameters including selenium, salinity, nitrate and sulfate in the lower Arkansas River. They developed a relationship between salinity and selenium that showed that some of the variation in selenium could be related to salinity.

Ortiz *et al.* (1998) also found that median dissolved selenium concentrations were generally largest during low flow conditions in the Arkansas River. Therefore, there is likely an inverse relationship between flow and dissolved selenium concentrations in the Arkansas River, a relationship also seen with salinity.

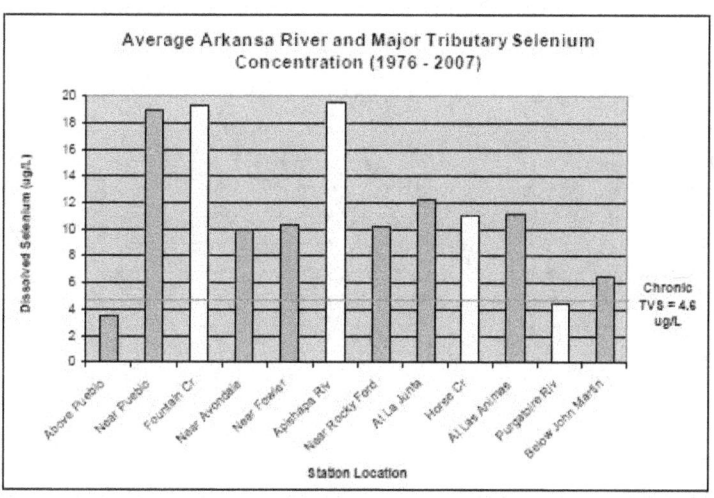

Figure 19. Selenium concentration in the Lower Arkansas River (upstream to downstream) and major tributaries (from Tetra Tech 2007). Mainstem locations are in blue and tributaries in yellow.

A substantial amount of the watershed of the lower Arkansas River drains over marine shale formations (see Figure 10). Donnelly and Gates (2005) stated that irrigation over soils derived from marine sedimentary rocks can accelerate dissolution and mobility of selenium into ground water and subsequently the Arkansas River. Additionally, crop irrigation increases the consumptive use in the watershed, concentrating dissolved constituents such as selenium. Ortiz *et al.* (1998) stated that local geology and irrigation return flows are the two most likely causes of the increasing selenium in the Arkansas River between Pueblo and Las Animas.

The lower Arkansas River is considered one of the most saline streams of its size in the U.S. due to excessive irrigation, seepage from earthen canals, inadequate drainage facilities, and a rising ground water table that leaches soluble salts (e.g. iron, sulfate, and selenium) from underlying geologic marine shale formations. Such conditions allow these salts to be concentrated in the soil and irrigation return flow. This high total dissolved solids concentration lowers the water quality of the Arkansas River downstream of La Junta (CDPHE 2002).

The most common measure of salinity [also referred to as total dissolved solids (TDS)] is specific conductance. It is a measure of the ability of water to conduct electrical current and its value is related to the type and concentration of ions in solution. Typically, TDS concentration is approximately 65 percent of the specific conductance (μS/cm), although site-specific relationships are usually more accurate. There is no water quality standard for salinity in the Arkansas River basin. EPA has set a secondary maximum concentration level (MCL) for drinking water of 500 mg/l TDS (approximately equal to 740 μS/cm specific conductance). Secondary MCLs are non-enforceable guidelines for contaminant levels at the tap.

The specific conductance of the lower Arkansas River generally increases downstream from Pueblo to Las Animas (Lewis 1998, MHW 2008, Figure 20). Specific conductance is also inversely related to flow, e.g. low flows in December have high specific conductance (Figure 21). The overall trend for specific conductance to increase downstream is due to the fact that irrigation-return flows compose an increasingly large percentage of stream flow.

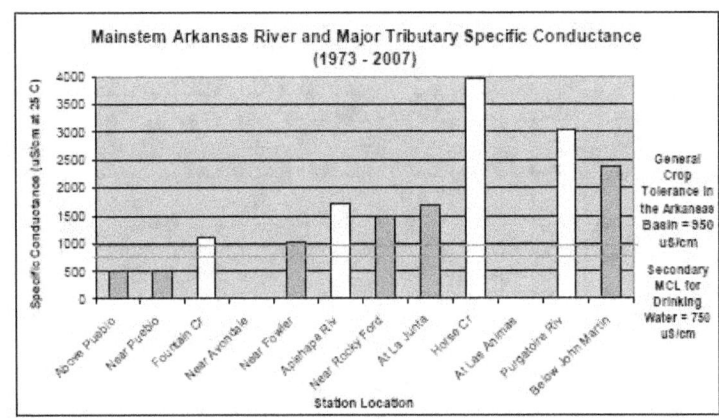

Figure 20. Specific conductance in the lower Arkansas River and major tributaries (from Tetra Tech 2007). Mainstem locations in blue; tributaries in yellow.

Total recoverable iron is an impairment in the COARLA01a segment of the lower Arkansas River (CDPHE 2006), as well as in previous 303 (d) listings for the COARLA01b segment.

Ortiz *et al.* (1998) noted elevated concentrations of total recoverable iron in the lower Arkansas River. They found that upstream of Las Animas, concentrations were substantially higher during snowmelt runoff and post-snowmelt runoff seasons. In addition, Ortiz *et al.* found that the major tributaries, such as the Apishapa River, had storm flow total iron concentrations 200-300 times the concentrations that occur in the Arkansas River mainstem –the likely source of iron in the lower Arkansas River are highly erosional tributaries.

Zielinski *et al.* (1995) studied dissolved uranium concentrations in the Arkansas River. They found that the rate of increase of dissolved uranium concentration with distance downriver increased markedly as the river flowed from predominately undeveloped lands underlain by igneous and metamorphic rocks to agriculturally developed lands underlain by marine shale and

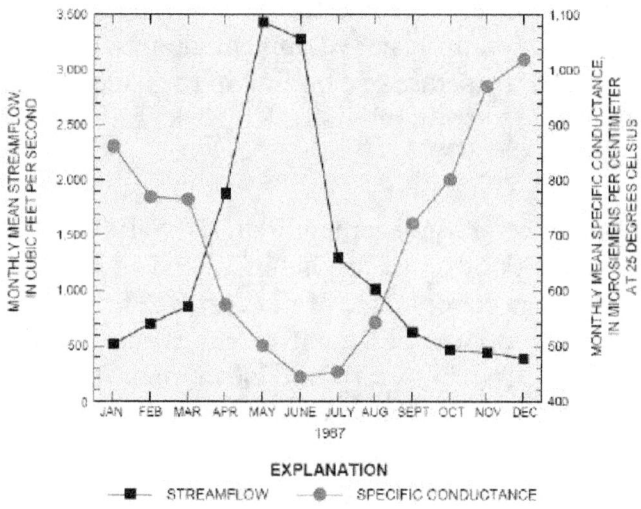

Figure 21. Seasonal relationship of stream flow to specific conductance for the Arkansas River near Avondale (Lewis1998).

limestone. Additionally, they observed an abrupt increase in dissolved uranium along that portion of the river where river discharge is substantially reduced due to irrigation diversions, and where remaining flow is largely composed of irrigation return water. Dissolved uranium concentrations in the river and most of its tributaries exceeded the U.S. drinking water standard of 20 μg/L. Uranium concentrations of river water from agricultural use areas showed a strong positive correlation with major dissolved constituents (e.g., sodium, calcium, magnesium and sulfate).

Ortiz *et al.* (1998) found that bacteria densities at sites on the Arkansas River generally increased in the downstream direction and that densities were generally low compared to the water quality standards. Also, from 1998-2004 no samples (n=41) from the Colorado Canal to John Martin Reservoir segment of the Arkansas River exceeded the fecal coliform water quality standard (MHW 2008). However, there is no longer a water quality standard for fecal coliform in the lower Arkansas River because the State of Colorado has transitioned to *E. coli*-based water quality standards (CDPHE 2007). There are limited *E. coli* data for stations in this segment, but the low densities of fecal coliform in the mainstem indicate that *E. coli* densities are also likely low in the Arkansas River.

Floodplains, Wetlands and Riparian Areas

Lower Arkansas River valley floods may be characterized as low density, long-duration rainfall over a large area, or short duration thunderstorms of high intensity rainfall over a small area. These localized events are common in southeast Colorado and account for the presence of arroyos and intermittent streams.

Floods on the Arkansas River are of two general types: spring floods result from snow melt and are often augmented by storm runoff, and summer floods result entirely from storm runoff. Spring floods are characterized by moderate flow of long duration with large volumes of runoff. Summer floods are characterized by high flow with relatively smaller volumes of runoff. Major floods along the Arkansas River occurred in July 1886, June 1921, May 1955, May 1969, and April 1999. Much of the Lower Arkansas River floodplain has been developed for agricultural purposes. Urban and residential development to the west of the NHS is also important with regard to flooding. The combination of this development along with the two major dams along the river has significantly altered the nature of flooding in the valley. In addition to the Arkansas floodplain, two local tributaries (upstream of NHS), King and Anderson arroyos, have previously contributed to significant floods.

According to the park's draft General Management Plan (NPS 1994), the Colorado Water Conservation Board reported the flood stage heights of 12 and 14 feet above the river channel for the 100- and 500-year floods, respectively. The water surface elevation of the 100-year flood is 4,002 ft NGVD (National Geodetic Vertical Datum) which is approximately the elevation of the lowest point of the fort grounds. The 500-year flood elevation is 4,004 feet NGVD; a flood of this elevation would completely inundate the fort.

The National Weather Service has developed the Advanced Hydrologic Prediction Service (http://water.weather.gov/ahps2/index.php?wfo=pub). The NHS is encouraged to consult this website, especially during the flood season, for predictions of flooding stage heights/flows. Figures 22 and 23 are representative website plots for the U.S. Geological Survey gage at La Junta. Figure 22 shows the stage heights from the previous three days as well as the forecasted stage heights for the next 5-day period. Figure 23 shows the chance of river stage exceeding various levels during the forecasted time period (in this case May 27 – September 23, 2010).

For such long-range forecasts, it should be expected that conditions will change over such extended periods. These forecasts are updated periodically and should be consulted on a regular basis.

Wetlands represent transitional environments between terrestrial and aquatic systems where the water table is at or near the surface or the land is covered by shallow water (Cowardin et al. 1979). Flora within these wetland systems exhibit extreme spatial variability, triggered by very slight changes in elevation. Temporal variability is also great because the surface water depth is highly influenced by changes in precipitation, evaporation and/or infiltration.

Cowardin et al. (1979) developed a wetland classification system that is now the standard in the federal government. In this system, a wetland must have one or more of the following attributes: (1) at least periodically, the land supports predominately hydrophytes; (2) the substrate is

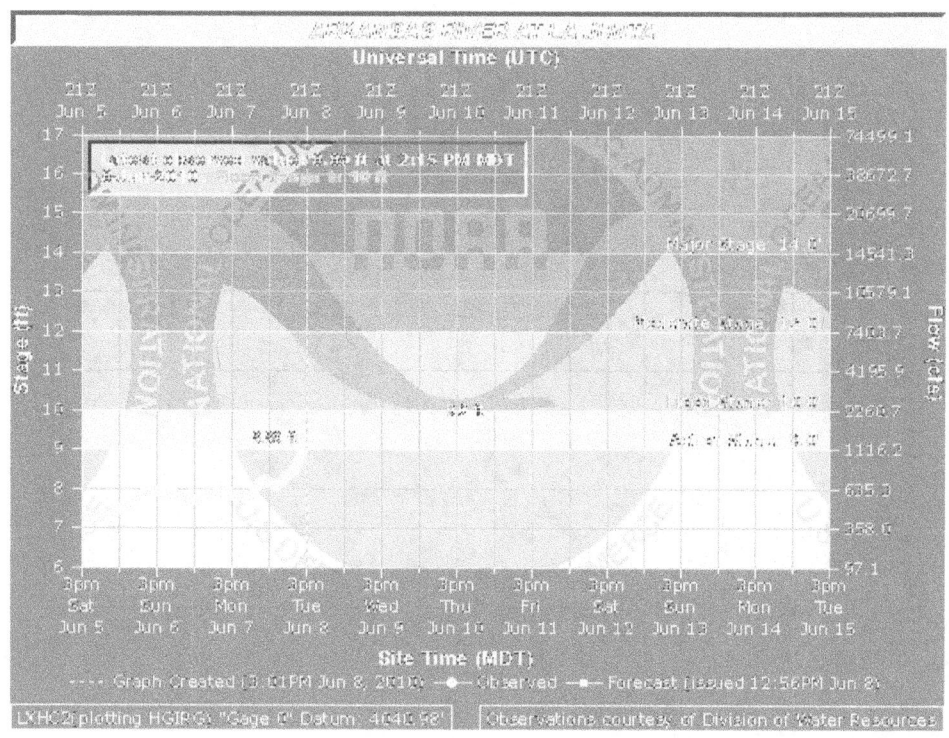

Figure 22. Plot from the National Weather Service's Advanced Hydrologic Prediction Service of actual and forecasted stage height and flow for the June 5-15, 2010 period for the La Junta gage (from (http://water.weather.gov/ahps2/hydrograph.php?wfo=pub&gage=lxhc2&view=1,1,1,1,1,1,1,1).

predominately un-drained hydric soil; and (3) the substrate is non-soil and is saturated with water or covered by shallow water at some time during the growing season of each year.

The National Wetlands Inventory map (Hadley Quadrangle) that includes the NHS identifies the following wetlands based on the Cowardin *et al*. (1977) classification system: 1) the Arkansas River is classified as a lower perennial, open water, riverine wetland; 2) south of the river there are palustrine, forested/scub/shrub (PFO/PSS) and forested/flat palustrine (PFO/PFL) wetlands; and, 3) north of the river there are PFO/PSS, PFO and palustrine, emergent (PEM) wetlands (see Figure 24).

Gionfriddo *et al*. (2002) conducted wetland plant surveys at the seven known wetlands in the NHS and found a total of 31 wetland species (the NHS now recognizes six wetlands; see Figure 24). Tisdale-Hein (2006) concentrated on only one wetland area (Arch Wetland). The wetland summaries below are taken from these two studies.

The Arch Wetland (PEM/PFO; Figure 24) is a 55-acre palustrine wetland located on the second floodplain bench of the Arkansas River that park natural resource staff has identified as one of the park's key natural resources. It is semi-permanently flooded, and is covered by a dense (approximately 90%), homogenous stand of cattails (*Typha latifolia*). In addition, cattail comprises at least 70 percent of the wet soil area around the wetland (Tisdale-Hein 2006). Open water areas in the wetland are few and water depth is around 18 inches. Cattails provide less quality habitat than the two bulrush species at the wetland [*Schoenoplectus lacustris acutus* (hardstem bulrush) and *Scirpus paludosus* (alkali bulrush)]. Water inflow to the wetland is from

43

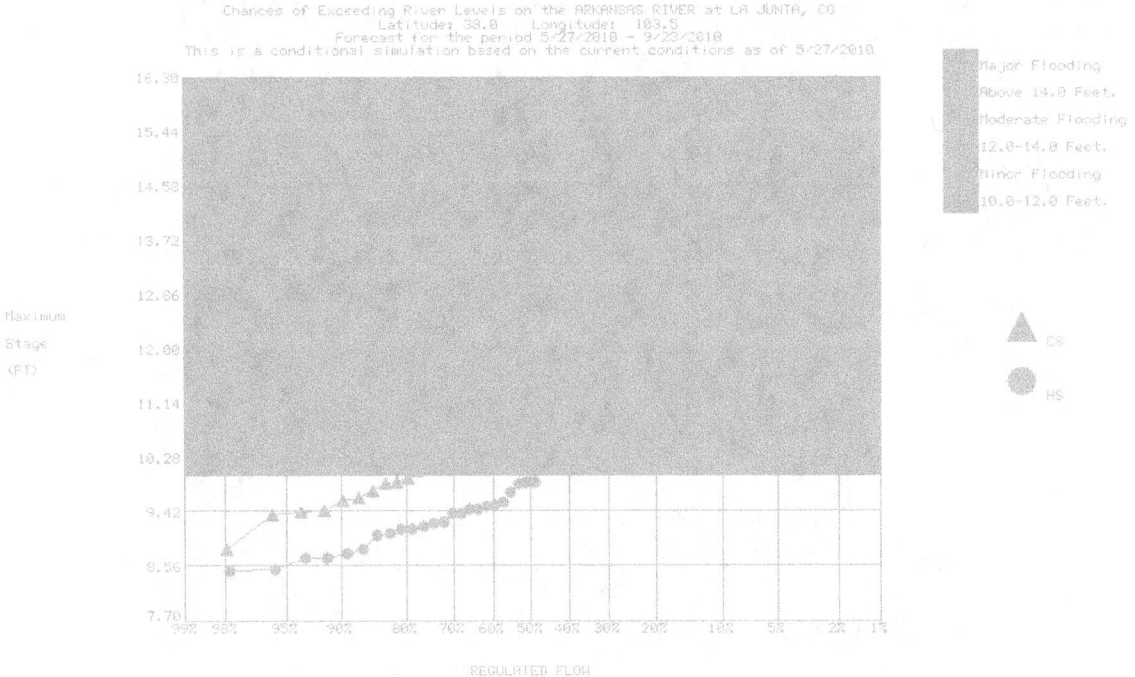

Figure 23. Plot from the National Weather Service's Advanced Hydrologic Prediction Service of river stage versus exceedance probability for the May 27-September 23, 2010 time period for La Junta gage (from http://water.weather.gov/ahps2/period.php?wfo=pub&gage=lxhc2&view=1,1,1,1,1,1,1,1&toggles=10,7,8,2,9,15,6). The conditional simulation (CS) line indicates the chances of the river exceeding given levels based on current levels. The historical simulation (HS) line indicates the chances of the river exceeding given levels based on the total range of past levels. For example, if the CS line is substantially above the HS line, the conditions are wetter than normal conditions and the chances are greater for wet conditions over the entire range; whereas, if the CS line is substantially below the HS line, the conditions are drier than normal conditions and the chances are greater for drier conditions over the entire range. When the CS and HS lines are very close across the entire range, the changes of the river exceeding a certain level is similar to the total range of past levels.

bank overflow from the Arkansas River and leakage from Fort Lyon Canal – it is this leakage and the concomitant water table rise that caused this wetland to increase in size during the 1980's and 1990's. This dependence means that any decrease in flow in the Fort Lyon canal could cause a decrease in the size of the Arch Wetland (Woods *et al.* 2002). In addition, upgradient groundwater withdrawals could reduce groundwater inflows and reduce the size of the wetland. The wetland has high flood attenuation and storage capability due to the dense vegetative cover and restricted outlet and its occurrence within the floodplain of the Arkansas River. Tisdale-Hein (2006) recorded 70 plant species from this wetland; 15 (22 percent) of these species are exotic. In contrast, Gionfriddo *et al.* (2002) recorded only 19 wetland plant species for this wetland. Tisdale-Hein noted habitat for beneficial species such as hardstem bulrush (*Schoenoplectus lacustris acutus*), alkali bulrush, prairie coneflower (*Ratibida tagetes*) and other natives, were found in Arch Wetland along with persistent exotic species such as tamarisk and Russian olive. Canada thistle (*Cirsium arvense*) is a major problem around the perimeter of the Arch Wetland and forms a monoculture in several areas, restricting riparian plant species diversity. Tisdale-Hein (2006) classified the overall health of the wetland as fair with limitations

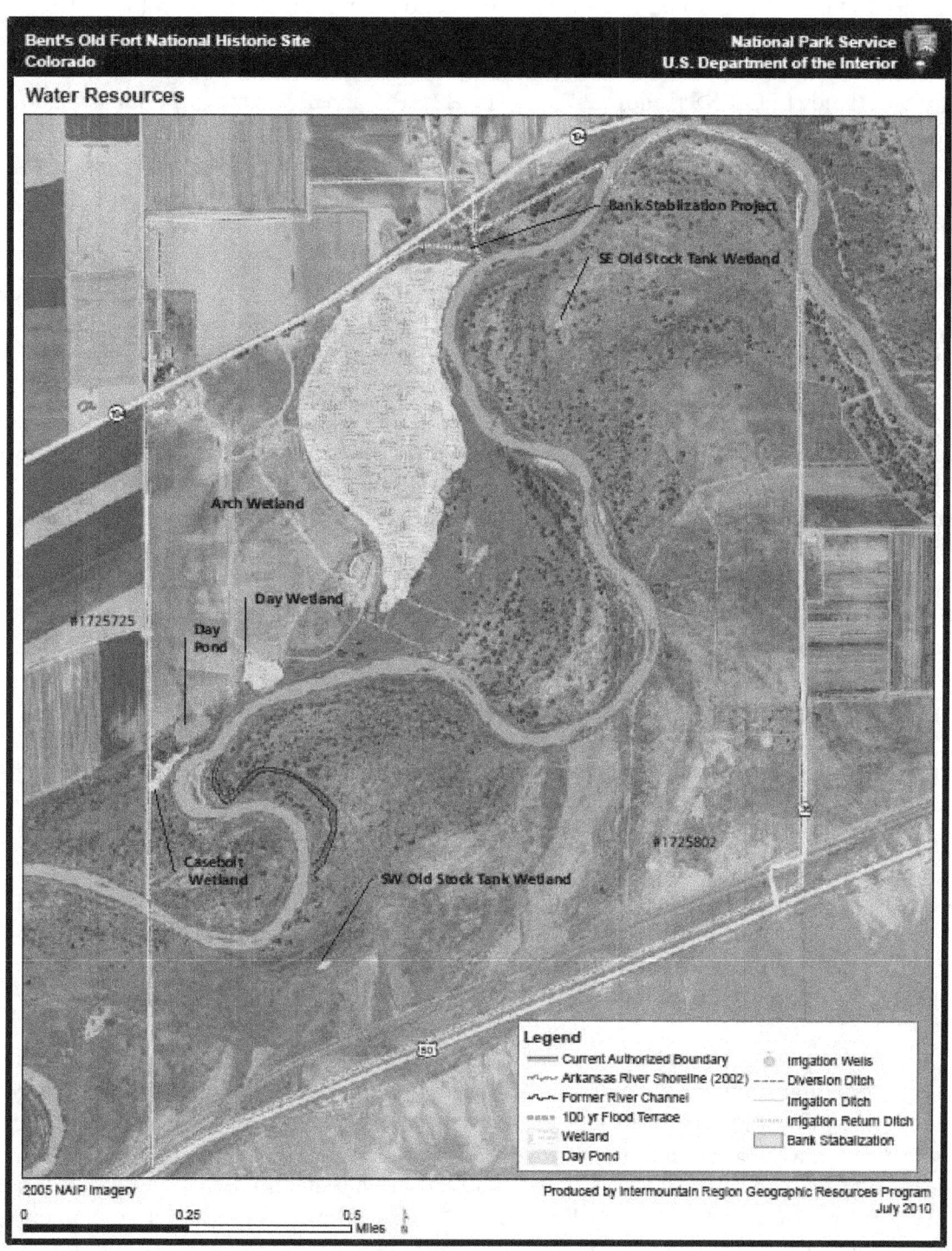

Figure 24. Locations of extant wetlands in Bent's Old Fort NHS. Arch Wetland corresponds to the PFO/PEM wetland on the NWI map; Casebolt wetland to PFO/PSS; SE Old Stock Tank wetland would be classified as PFO/PSS; the SW Old Stock Tank wetland corresponds to PFO/PFL; the Day Wetland and the Day Pond, although not delineated on the NWI map, are both PEM/OW wetlands with the Day Pond being more open water than the Day Wetland. The seventh wetland identified by Gionfriddo *et al.* (2002) occupied the former river channel. The Bank Stabilization project mitigated an erosion (head cut) problem in the irrigation return ditch just before it empties into the Arkansas River.

45

involving the monocultures of cattail and thistle, shallow depth of the open water areas, and the possible anaerobic conditions within the wetlands.

Case bolt Wetland (PFO/PSS; Figure 24) is a small (> 0.5 acres), open water, palustrine wetland located 100 feet south of the Day Pond. During their survey, Gionfriddo et al. (2002) found that this wetland had open, shallow water; soils indicated that the wetland is permanently inundated. Plant species such as wild licorice, vine mesquite, pondweed, and cattails are found here. The source of water is likely from irrigation water overflow from an adjacent culvert or seepage from the Day Pond. Gionfriddo et al. noted that this wetland had experienced low water or was almost dry for a few years prior to their survey – probably affected by the dynamic interactions of the Arkansas River, alluvial aquifer and the Fort Lyons Canal. This wetland was classified by Gionfriddo et al. as a small pondweed (*Potamogeton foliosus*) type of wetland and they found a total of 11 wetland plant species.

The Day Wetland (PEM/OW; Figure 24) is an excavated wetland south of the fort. There is no hydrologic connection to the Arkansas River. Vegetation is dominated by cattails and hard stem bulrush with 13 wetland plant species (Gionfriddo et al. 2002).

Day Pond (PEM/OW; Figure 24) is an open water wetland just south of the fort. It was probably a man-made irrigation retention pond because it is deep with steep sides. Hardstem bulrush and cattails dominated the vegetation; Gionfriddo et al. (2002) found 15 wetland plant species. It was considered for removal in the late 1990's, but was kept because of wildlife study opportunities and as a water source for fire suppression.

The Southwest Old Stock Tank wetland (PFO/PFL; Figure 24) is a depression that likely receives overflow from the Arkansas River during large flooding events. A total of 10 plant species was found for this wetland.

The Southeast Old Stock Tank wetland (PFO/PSS; Figure 24), is an old river channel depression in which a man-made stock tank was excavated circa 1940s-1950s supporting the occurrence of cattails; however no open water was observed (Gionfriddo et al. 2002). A total of seven wetland plant species was observed by Gionfriddo et al.

Natural riparian zones are some of the most diverse, dynamic, and complex biophysical habitats in the terrestrial environment (Naiman et al. 1993). The riparian zone encompasses that stream channel between low and high watermarks and that portion of the terrestrial landscape from the high watermark toward the uplands where vegetation may be influenced by elevated water tables or flooding and by the ability of the soils to hold water (Naiman and Decamps 1997). Thus, riparian zones may be classified as wetlands or, at the least, have a significant portion existing as wetland. Riparian zones are key systems for regulating aquatic-terrestrial linkages (Ward 1998) and they may provide early indications of environmental change (Decamps 1993).

Physically, riparian zones control mass movements of materials and channel morphology (Naiman and Decamps 1997). Ecologically, riparian zones: 1) provide sources of nourishment – terrestrial inputs to rivers; 2) control nonpoint sources of pollution, in particular, sediment and nutrients in agricultural watersheds; and 3) create a complex of shifting habitats (both in time and space), through variations in flood duration and frequency and concomitant changes in water table depth and plant succession (Naiman and Decamps 1997).

The riparian zone along the Arkansas River at the NHS, prior to 2004, consisted of cottonwoods, with willow and tamarisk. The cottonwoods were established during the historic period when the river experienced periodic flooding. Stands of willow occur along the river banks and help delineate earlier or additional stream channels. Dense stands of tamarisk were established in the early part of the 20th century and in some areas overtook the native willow stands, greatly affecting willow regeneration. Regeneration of the cottonwoods is not naturally occurring because of the change in the hydrology of the river; the cottonwood stand is mature and dying out.

In 2004, the NHS eliminated all standing tamarisk (*T. ramosissima*) from the Arkansas River riparian area within its boundary – a total of 350 acres of tamarisk was removed. This removal has facilitated willow regeneration. Controlling tamarisk required cutting trees to within 6 inches of the ground and applying herbicide to the stumps. The NHS is assisted by the Chihuahuan Desert-Southern Shortgrass Prairie Exotic Plant Management Team in the continued control of tamarisk re-sprouting.

Tamarisk is a facultative phreatophyte with an extensive root system that allows it to effectively exploit many of the degraded conditions along southwestern river systems today (e.g. interrupted flow regimes, reduced flooding, increased fire). Once a tamarisk stand is mature, it will remain the dominant feature of an ecosystem unless removed by human means. Tamarisk has a higher tolerance of fire, drought, and salinity than native species. It can increase fire frequency and intensity, drought, and salinity of a site. Hence, a strong initial infestation will promote a positive feedback mechanism that will lead to more tamarisk invasion (www.tamariskcoalition.org).

In 2007, a partnership formed to develop a strategic plan for Colorado's Arkansas River riparian areas impacted by non-native invasive trees, principally tamarisk and Russian olive. This partnership, known as the Arkansas River Watershed Invasive Plants Plan (ARKWIPP) includes the NHS.

The Colorado Division of Wildlife has launched a riparian mapping web page (http://ndis1.nrel.colostate.edu/riparian/riparian.htm). This website highlights the Division's Colorado Riparian Vegetation Mapping Project, whose goal is to develop a statewide data layer of riparian vegetation for use in natural resource planning applications. The generation of the riparian data layer in the vicinity of the NHS has been completed.

AQUATIC BIOLOGICAL RESOURCES

Water-based Birds

There are 72 species of birds listed for the NHS in the NPSpecies database. There is relatively little information regarding entirely water-based bird species, and the NHS could benefit from an avian survey during the migratory season. Giondfriddo *et al.* (2002) documented the presence of the great blue heron (*Ardea herodias*), green heron (*Butorides virescens*), and mallard (*Anas platyrhynchos*). In a follow-up bird survey, Gionfriddo and Stevens (2003) found the following additional water-based bird species: black-crowned night heron (*Nycticorax nycticorax*); white-faced ibis (*Plegadis chihi*); blue-winged teal (*Anas discors*); cinnamon teal (*Anas cyanoptera*); northern shoveler (*Anas clypeata*); Forster's tern (*Sterna forsteri*); black tern (*Chlidonias niger*); and American Avocet (*Recurvirostra americana*)

Water-based Mammals

Most mammals at the NHS are primarily land-based species with two exceptions, the American beaver (*Castor canadensis*) and the common muskrat (*Ondatra zibethicus*). These species have been observed on an occasional basis (Gionfriddo *et al.* 2002) but little is known about current population size.

Fish

Two fish surveys (Table 3) have been performed within the NHS in 2001 (Gionfriddo *et al.* 2002) and 2005 (Tisdale-Hein 2006). Based on these studies, 13 species of fish have been collected thus far in NHS waters. Gionfriddo *et al.* sampled via dip nets, seines and direct observation; however, sampling of fishes occurred only at the Day Pond and Arch Wetland. Because of the limited, sampling only four species of fish were collected. The only fish species of concern present at BEOL is the flathead chub. It is not known how abundant the flathead chub population is in the vicinity of the park. Tisdale-Hein collected a total of 12 species of fish; nine species from the Arkansas River and three species from the Arch wetland. Fish were collected via 15 minnow traps (10 in the river and 5 in Arch Wetland) that represented 1050 trap-hours. In the Arkansas River, fish were also sampled using dip netting and seines.

It is also interesting to look at species collected by habitat. For example, Gionfriddo *et al.* (2002) found only common carp at the Day Pond. In contrast, a sampling of the Day Pond in 2005 by a group of science teachers found four species: red shiner; mosquitofish; green sunfish; and bullhead catfish (*Ameriurus* sp.) (Fran Pannebaker, pers. comm., Bent's Old Fort NHS 2006). Similarly, Gionfriddo *et al.* and Tisdale-Hein (2006) each found three species at the Arch Wetland, but only two were in common. The two additional species, green sunfish and brook stickleback, represent a habitat generalist and a habitat specialist, respectively. Such differences in species collected from floodplain habitats are to be expected and depend on the extent of upstream flooding, the extent of and amount of time for local inundation, the mobility of various species, and sampling methodology.

The flathead chub and suckermouth minnow (*Phenacobius mirabilis*) are the only species of conservation concern (Colorado state species of concern and Colorado endangered, respectively) that occur within the NHS; both are resident species of the Arkansas River. It was suspected that the Arkansas darter (*Etheostoma cragini*; federal candidate species and state threatened) may be present in park waters. In fact, a main objective of the surveys by Gionfriddo *et al.* (2002) and Tisdale-Hein (2006) was to determine the presence of the darter. However, there is no suitable habitat for this darter species in NHS waters (Tisdale-Hein 2006, D. Vana-Miller, pers. obs.)

Amphibians and Reptiles

Thirteen species of reptile have been documented at the park: two turtles, spiny softshell turtle (*Apalone spinifera*) and snapping turtle (*Chelydra serpentine*); three lizards, Texas horned lizard (*Phrynosoma cornutum*), Great Plains skink (*Eumeces obsoletus*), and six-lined racerunner

Table 3. Fish species collected at Bent's Old Fort National Historic Site by three studies. The 24 species in the left column are from the NPSpecies database and represent those expected to be present in the NHS' waters. However, NPSpecies lists 26 species – two species (red shiner and flathead chub) are listed twice because of taxonomic changes in genus names. The study by Nesler *et al.* (1999) represents a larger reach that includes the NHS. 'X' means collected.

Scientific Name	Common Name	Gionfriddo *et al.* (2002)	Tisdale-Hein (2006)	Nesler *et al.* (1999)
Dorosoma cepedianum	gizzard shad			X
Catosmus catostomus	longnose sucker			X
Catostomus commersoni	white sucker			X
Campostoma anomalum	central stoneroller			X
Cyprinella lutrensis	red shiner		X	X
Cyprinus carpio	common carp	X		X
Platygobio gracilis	flathead chub		X	X
Notropis stramineus	sand shiner		X	X
Phenacobius mirabilis	suckermouth minnow		X	X
Pimephales promelas	fathead minnow		X	X
Rhinichthys cataractae	longnose dace			
Fundulus zebrinus	plains killifish	X	X	X
Gambusia afffinis	mosquitofish	X	X	
Culaea inconstans	brook stickleback		X	
Lepomis cyanellus	green sunfish	X		X
Lepomis humilis	orangespotted sunfish			X
Lepomis macrochirus	bluegill		X	
Micropterus salmoides	largemouth bass			X
Pomoxis annularis	white crappie			X
Pomoxis nigromaculatus	black crappie			X
Perca flavescens	yellow perch			X
Sander vitreus X Sander canadense	walleye X sauger hybrid			X
Ameriurus melas	black bullhead			
Ameiurus nebulosus	brown bullhead		X[1]	

Ictalurus punctatus	channel catfish		X	

1 Study noted specimens collected as *Ameiurus* sp. with no identification to species.

(*Cnemidophorus sexlineatus*); and eight snakes, bullsnake (*Pituophis catenifer*), plains garter snake (*Thamnophis radix*), prairie rattlesnake (*Crotalus viridis*), plains black-headed snake (*Tantilla nigriceps*), Great Plains ratsnake (*Elaphe guttata emoryi*), coachwhip (*Masticophis flagellum*), western hognose snake (*Heterodon nasicus*), and northern water snake (*Nerodia sipedon*) (Gionfriddo *et al.* 2002). However, of these reptiles only the spiny softshell and snapping turtles are considered aquatic. Only three amphibian species have been documented: the Woodhouse's toad (*Bufo woodhousii*), plains leopard frog (*Rana blairi*; Colorado State species of concern), and the American bullfrog (*Rana catesbeiana*) (Gionfriddo *et al.* 2002; Gionfriddo and Stevens 2003). Park staff have observed the presence of tiger salamanders (*Ambystoma tigrinum*), but the presence of predatory fish at the NHS wetland sites probably precludes successful reproduction of this species (Gionfriddo and Stevens 2003). Additionally, Gionfriddo *et al.* (2002) speculated that spadefoot toads (*Scaphiopus* sp. and *Spea* sp.) may be present but the timing of their survey did not coincide with the period of intense breeding activity for these species.

Drinking Water

Treated drinking water is supplied to the NHS via underground piping by Bent's Fort Water Company (BFWC), located in La Junta, CO. BFWC has operated as many as six ground water wells in North La Junta. It currently operates one ground water well in North La Junta; this well is classified as a small public water supply, serving approximately 900 residents. The company purchases 50 percent of its water from the City of La Junta; when this last well fails, the company will purchase all of its water from the city. Over the past 10 years, BFWC has accrued numerous violations under the Safe Drinking Water Act for untimely monitoring of its wells.

As the water from BFWC enters the NHS water room, a hypo-chlorination treatment system injects sodium hypochlorite solution into the source water as it flows to the storage tank. A pump facility takes suction from the storage tank and with the assistance of two pressure tanks, pressurizes a low flow reverse osmosis treatment system and the distribution system which supplies the buildings of the NHS. In addition, a custom bottled water treatment facility (low-flow) is operated to fill five gallon bottles for use in cooled drinking water dispensers by park staff.

Contaminants detected in BEOL drinking water, tested at the well source, are: barium, fluoride, nitrates/nitrites, copper, lead, radionuclides, sodium and total dissolved solids (TDS). Contaminants that exceeded the EPA maximum contaminant levels (MCL) are radium (226 and 228 combined), and total dissolved solids in all wells. The MCL's for TDS are secondary levels and are therefore non-enforceable standards set for aesthetic reasons. Elevated levels of radium are possibly caused by erosion and decay of natural deposits in the area. Surface and ground water around the NHS are known to have high levels of sodium and selenium due to irrigation and natural deposits in shale formations (see *Hydrogeology* section).

Bent's Old Fort National Historic Site is required to perform additional testing of its drinking and potable water, as it is considered a non-residential, non-transient water supplier. Water is tested the first Monday of each month, for compliance with state and federal standards. Water samples from the maintenance building and the fort itself are sent to the county health department in Pueblo, CO. Samples are tested for both types of coliform bacteria and *E. coli*; no violations have been reported.

Water Resource Issues and Recommendations

Staff from the NHS identified the following water resource issues:

- Water rights
- High water table – impacts to the fort
- High water table monitoring wells and future monitoring
- Irrigation wells
- Fire-supply wells
- Non-potable water wells
- Drinking water
- Arkansas River water quality and quantity
- Flooding
- Hazardous substances and spill prevention
- Wetland and riparian protection – water quality and quantity
- Storm drainage issue
- Sewage treatment and septic fields
- Man-made pond and stock tanks

We have consolidated the above list in the following discussion of the water resource issues and our recommendations.

Water Rights and Ground Water Wells

The Bent brother's irrigation project withdrawing water from the Arkansas River in the early 1830's is one of the earliest examples of appropriating water from Colorado's streams (Radosevich *et al.* 1976). Diverting and putting water to use is considered a basic right in the State and that right is incorporated in the Colorado Constitution. Article XVI § 5 states: "The water of every natural stream, not heretofore appropriated, within the State of Colorado, is hereby declared to be the property of the public, and the same is dedicated to the use of the people of the state, subject to appropriation as hereinafter provided." The Constitution further states "The right to divert the unappropriated waters of any natural stream to beneficial uses shall never be denied."

Colorado follows the doctrine of prior appropriation which applies to all surface water and groundwater tributary to surface water. The application of this doctrine is commonly summarized as "first in time, first in right" whereby senior (earlier priority date) water right holders on a stream system have priority to use the water over junior users when there is not enough water to supply all users. That is, senior users may use their full entitlement before the next junior user may divert any water.

A water right is limited to that amount of water put to beneficial use by an appropriator. The Colorado Statutes state: "Beneficial use is the use of that amount of water that is reasonable and appropriate under reasonably efficient practices to accomplish without waste the purpose for which the diversion is lawfully made and without limiting the generality of the foregoing, shall include the impoundment of water for recreational purposes, including fishery or wildlife." [Colo. Rev. Stats., §37-92-103(7)].

Water rights in Colorado are regulated by the Division of Water Resources; also known as the State Engineer's Office. Besides administering water rights, this office issues water well permits, monitors stream flow and water use, performs dam safety inspections, maintains databases of Colorado water information, and represents Colorado in interstate water compact proceedings (State of Colorado, 2008).

All water matters including determination of water rights are within the jurisdiction of the State water courts. Each water court has jurisdiction over one of the seven major river basins in the State. The Arkansas River Basin is within the jurisdiction of Water Division 2.

To acquire a water right, a water user may apply for a conditional water right, which allows the user to work towards perfecting the right with reasonable diligence while maintaining the priority date of the permit application. Once the diversion works are complete and water is put to beneficial use, the Water Court may decree the water right as absolute.

Water use from wells can be classified as exempt or non-exempt. Exempt wells are exempt from water rights administration (no permitting or perfecting process required) and are not included in the priority system. Non-exempt wells require permits and are administered in the priority system.

In 1948, the States of Kansas and Colorado signed a water rights compact concerning stream flow in the Arkansas River. The purpose of the compact is to settle disputes over flow entitlement and to equitably divide and apportion the waters of the Arkansas River between users within the two states. In the past, Kansas has not received all the water to which it was entitled under the compact and Kansas sued Colorado for damages. As a result, Colorado now regulates water use in the Arkansas River Basin very closely and no new depletions to river flow can occur unless the water withdrawn is replaced. New depletions and junior depletions that will cause Colorado to not meet its obligation to Kansas are called "out-of-priority depletions" by the State. The method for replacing out-of-priority depletions is documented in a Plan of Augmentation approved by the Water Court and often involves purchasing water from senior water right holders who are willing to sell or lease water (State of Colorado 2008). If the NHS requires additional water to meet its needs, the park will be required to have a Plan of Augmentation accepted by the Water Court.

The NPS, Water Resources Division, Water Rights Branch is the repository for the NPS water right dockets. These dockets contain relevant materials related to NPS water rights such as applications, permits, licenses, land transfer information, maps, water use submissions, and correspondence. The amount of material in each docket is variable, may contain out-of-date information, and some are incomplete. The following are brief summaries of the status of the NHS water rights found in the water right dockets:

- **BEOL 001** – Point of Diversion: NW¼ SW¼, Sec. 14, T23S, R54W, 6th P.M. This well is noted as "Well No. 1" or "Federal No. 1" in the water rights dockets. An application for a water right permit was filed for this well in 1966 for 100 gallons per minute for fire protection and irrigation purposes. No other documentation exists as to whether a permit was granted or not. A hand-written note in the files states "Well not in use, 1987." A

June 22, 1994 memorandum from the Chief, Water Rights Branch to the BEOL Superintendent states (referring to Wells 1 and 2) "These wells are abandoned, no water right exist."

- **BEOL 002** – Point of Diversion: SE¼ SW¼, Sec. 14, T23S, R54W, 6th P.M. This well is noted as "Well No. 2" or "Federal No. 2" in the water rights dockets. A water right was acquired for 135 gallons per minute for fire protection and irrigation purposes from J.H. and Martha L. Baldridge. As stated in the Water Referee's ruling (Case No. 80CW142, dated May 13, 1987), the United States withdrew any claim to water from BEOL Well No. 2. A June 22, 1994 memorandum from the Chief, Water Rights Branch to the NHS Superintendent states (referring to Wells 1 and 2) "These wells are abandoned, no water right exist."

- **BEOL 003** – Point of Diversion: SW¼ SW¼, Sec. 14, T23S, R54W, 6th P.M. This well is noted as "Well No. 3" or "Federal No. 3" in the water right dockets. This is an absolute right and consists of Permit No. 201492 for 10 gpm for drinking and sanitation purposes and Permit 201493 for 140 gpm for fire-fighting purpose. The priority date for both permits is April 1, 1965. These permits are classified as "exempt" under Colorado Statute 37-92-602. As a result of this classification, this well is exempt from having to replace out-of-priority depletions to the Arkansas River system as described in the Amended Rules and Regulations Governing the Division and Use of Tributary Groundwater in the Arkansas River Basin, Colorado, approved September 27, 1995.

- **BEOL 004** – Point of Diversion: SW¼ SW¼, Sec. 14, T23S, R54W, 6th P.M (see Figure 24). This well is noted as "Irrigation Well" or "Federal No. 4" in the water right dockets and the "Day Well" by the NHS staff. This is an absolute underground right for 720 gpm (not to exceed 153 acre-feet per year) for irrigation purposes with a priority date of January 30, 1954. A 1995 document shows that the NHS transmitted monthly electric meter readings (from November, 1994 through October, 1995) and the total volume of water pumped to the State for this well. The 1974 Water Referee's ruling (W-3016) states the well number is RF-653, a replacement for 013596-F. No permits are found in the water rights dockets.

In the mid-1990s, the NHS proposed a project to revegetate certain lands (the old Day property) with native vegetation. Since they wanted to use water from this well, a plan of Augmentation was required to replace the out-of-priority depletion to the Arkansas River system as described in the Amended Rules and regulations Governing the Division and Use of Tributary Groundwater in the Arkansas River Basin, Colorado, approved September 27, 1995.

The NHS eventually contracted with the Colorado Water Protective and Development Association who in turn supplied water to the river to augment the park's out-of-priority depletion from their approved Augmentation Plan. In 1997, the NHS used 160 acre-feet per year (afy) to irrigate 40 acres, but reduced that amount to 20 afy in approximately 2000. The park ceased using this water after 2009 (Fran Pannebaker, Bent's Old Fort NHS, pers. comm., September 2008).

- **BEOL 005** – Point of Diversion: SE¼ SE¼, Sec. 23, T23S, R54W, 6th P.M. This well is noted as "Livestock Well" in the water right dockets. A well abandonment affidavit states the well was plugged and abandoned on December 13, 1989.

- **BEOL 006** - Point of Diversion: SE¼ NE¼, Sec. 23, T23S, R54W, 6th P.M (see Figure 24). This well is noted as "Harmon Property" in the water right dockets. Well Registration No. 156062-A was issued on December 13, 1989 for this well. A Notice of Inactive Well form, which was likely submitted to the Division Engineer, is found in the docket stating the well was disconnected from its power supply. The notice is signed by the BEOL Superintendent on June 13, 1995. It is an exempt well as classified by the State of Colorado. As a result of this classification, this well is exempt from having to replace out-of-priority depletions to the Arkansas River system as described in the Amended Rules and regulations governing the Division and Use of Tributary Groundwater in the Arkansas River Basin, Colorado, approved September 27, 1995.

  The NHS is interested in restoring approximately 100 acres of land south of the Arkansas River to native vegetation. Recently, it was suggested that the park request the CWPDA to transfer the 20 afy associated with BEOL 004 to BEOL 006 for the purposes of irrigating this land during the restoration process (Hughes 2010).

The NHS has the rights to 47 shares in the Fort Lyons Canal Company acquired from Barbara Day and Robert and Evelyn Wilburn for irrigation purposes. These shares equate to 0.47 cubic feet per second of water from the Company. Park staff state that the park has never used this water (Fran Pannebaker, Bent's Old Fort NHS, pers. comm. September 2008). Hughes (2010) mentioned that a possible near-term use of these shares could be for irrigation of the native vegetation restoration on NHS lands south of the Arkansas River. In this case the NHS could offer the CWPDA all or part of its 47 shares; the CWPDA would then evaluate the shares and determine the amount of ground water that the shares represent. This ground water could then be pumped from one of the existing wells for irrigation purposes.

Recommendations
The water rights information described above should be updated to fill in missing information as to the history and present status of NHS water rights for both the park files and Water Rights Branch dockets. In order to accomplish this task, files from the Colorado Division of Water Resources, Fort Lyon Canal Company, and the Colorado Water Court should be reviewed and copies made of missing information for each well and ditch right. Submitting a Technical Assistance request to the NPS, Water Resources Division is an option if NHS does not have the staff or expertise in this matter. Also, an analysis should be made by the park as to its current and future water needs to determine if existing NHS water rights are adequate. If certain wells and/or water rights are no longer needed, an effort to properly abandon the well(s) and right(s) should be undertaken. Since more irrigation use is planned for other areas of the NHS, an effort should be made to see if the NHS shares in the Fort Lyons Canal Company could be exchanged for the right to divert tributary ground water from the Arkansas River basin.

Water Quality and Quantity of the Arkansas River

Two of the three water-based vital signs of the SOPN are surface water quality and quantity. Texas State University (2007), working for the SOPN, reviewed available surface water information in network parks and provided the following recommendations for the NHS:

- Water quality data collected since the early 1990s should be compiled, incorporated into the historical database, and analyzed for water quality condition and trends, particularly for U.S. Geological Survey gaging station on the Arkansas River at Hadley, CO (USGS #07123300) commonly referred to as station BEOL 7 (see NPS 1998);
- Routine (weekly) water quality monitoring of vital sign core constituents (water temperature, dissolved oxygen, pH, specific conductance and indicator bacteria) should be conducted at BEOL 7. This should be supplemented by seasonal, continuous (diel) monitoring of DO and pH to provide additional understanding of river chemical conditions. Consideration should also be given to monthly monitoring of nutrient concentrations and major ions (e.g., sulfate and total dissolved solids);
- Annual or seasonal monitoring of aquatic biological condition (primarily macroinvertebrates) because aquatic biota integrate water quality conditions over time.

Recommendations

NPS (1998) provided a basic retrospective analysis of water quality conditions at those monitoring stations with records in STORET, the national water quality database. In our estimation that analysis was and is of limited value to the NHS, simply because the closest upstream station with an adequate period of record is in La Junta, 8 miles west of the NHS. The closest downstream station is on the Arkansas River at Hadley, CO (USGS #07123300 and BEOL 7), two miles downstream. However, that station has been inactive since the 1980's and has a very limited period of record that did not measure discharge. This station would not be viable for any retrospective water quality analysis, let alone any current monitoring. The La Junta station (USGS #07123000) has an adequate period of record (in some cases > 50 years and current) for most of the five core water quality vital signs. Additionally, other important constituents (e.g. calcium, sulfate, selenium) also have adequate periods of record. Most importantly, discharge is measured at this station. Because there are no permanent water inputs to the Arkansas River between La Junta and the NHS, the analysis of water quality data from the La Junta station would provide useful information. We recommend that the NHS submit a technical assistance request to the NPS Water Resources Division for a status and trends analysis of water quality and discharge information for the La Junta station.

Similarly, the establishment of any routine water quality monitoring at the Hadley station would also be problematic. We recommend two options for the establishment of routine water quality monitoring of the Arkansas River at the NHS. First, the SOPN could establish a core vital signs monitoring site just downstream of the west boundary of the NHS; a quarterly sampling frequency would be the minimum. These water quality data could be correlated with the discharge data of the La Junta station. Additionally, the network could data mine the La Junta site for other important constituents. Second, the network or NHS could totally rely on data mining of discharge and water quality data from the La Junta station.

Routine monitoring of biological condition is an important tool in understanding overall water resource condition. Because the sampling, identification, and analysis of the aquatic macroinvertebrate community require specialized expertise, we do not recommend this as something to be accomplished by the NHS. The SOPN would be the NPS entity better suited for the lead in such an assessment; however, understanding aquatic biological condition is not a SOPN vital sign, and may be of low priority.

Colorado's Ecological Monitoring and Assessment Program (EMAP) within the Colorado Department of Public Health and the Environment developed bioassessment tools for use in monitoring and assessing streams statewide. Specifically, that program developed a benthic macroinvertebrate multimetric index for streams and rivers in the plains region of Colorado (CDPHE No Date; www.cdphe.state.co.us/wq/WaterShed/ColoradoEMAPReport.pdf). Multimetric indices (MMI) allow multiple biological measurements or metrics to be combined into a single unitless index value. Metrics are attributes of the biological assemblage, which can be quantified as a response to human and natural alteration or stress of the environment. MMIs are calibrated using reference conditions. By incorporating metrics representing species richness, species composition, functional feeding group, and pollution tolerance of benthic communities, MMIs can accurately indicate macroinvertebrate community health. The metrics involved in this index and the associated ecological categories are:

Metric	Category
Percent Chironomidae	Composition
EPT Taxa	Richness
Hilsenhoff Biotic Index	Tolerance
Percent Burrowers	Habit
Percent Predators	Trophic

In addition, a fish-based MMI was developed for Colorado plains rivers and streams (CDPHE no date) that included the following metrics:

Metric
Number of nonnative individuals
Percent of species that are native herbivores
Percent of hider individuals
Percent of native species that are long-lived and tolerant to sediment
Percent of native individuals that prefer warm-water habitats
Number of individuals that are benthic and tolerant to sediment

Paul *et al.* (2005) recommended that the State of Colorado implement the use of these MMIs to assess biological condition in streams and rivers of the plains. To our knowledge the State has not done so. One reason may be that these plains MMIs were constructed with very few reference (n=6) and stressed (n=3) sites. As a result, little of the true natural variation in metric values was characterized. Thus, their applicability is limited until verified with an independent set of data or recalibrated with larger sample sizes.

We recommend that the NHS contact the Colorado Department of Public Health and the Environment and propose that the State sample the Arkansas River macroinvertebrate community within the boundaries of the NHS as an additional stressed site. This would be a limited assessment to assist the State with refining the plains MMI. For the long-term, perhaps the NHS and State could develop a Memorandum of Agreement for the State to monitor the macroinvertebrate community in the Arkansas River at the NHS using the plains MMI on a recurring basis as part of a statewide assessment of stream biological condition. The same could be said for the fish-based MMI.

High Water Table and Impacts to the Bent's Old Fort

The study by Woods *et al.* (2002), although limited in scope and duration, provided the likely scientific basis for flooding of the Fort's basement. They believed that the primary control on ground water levels in the area around the NHS is the ground water flow from adjacent uplands, and the amount of this flow is dependent on the amount of excess irrigation and leakage from the Fort Lyon Canal. Under low to average flow conditions in the Arkansas River, the ground water gradient towards the river is maintained – the river reach through the NHS is maintained as a gaining reach. Under high flow conditions in the Arkansas River, a local reversal of the hydraulic gradient can occur such that ground water flows away from the river (and towards the Fort) and the river reach through the NHS is now a losing reach. They observed that the basement flooding in 1999 was associated with a peak flow in the Arkansas River that was twice as large as the second largest peak flow recorded since closure of the Pueblo Dam in 1974. The river stage in 1999 was more than 2.1 m higher than the peak flow in 2001 (year of study). Such high flows in Arkansas River could lead to a reversal in the hydraulic gradient. Woods *et al.* concluded that the flow of water from the river combined with increased leakage from the canal were the likely cause of the high water table levels and subsequent basement flooding in the fort.

Additionally, high river stage may only reduce the overall groundwater gradient and hamper drainage of water seeping from the Fort Lyon Canal (Woods *et al.* 2002). In particular, water flooding the basement may indeed be coming from the canal rather than the Arkansas River, but the net result is the same. Woods *et al.* believed that a more detailed term study of different water sources and aquifer properties would be needed to evaluate the effect of the river, the canal and excess irrigation on water table elevations and basement flooding at the Fort.

Recommendations

Given that ground water quantity is a vital sign of the SOPN, we agree with the recommendations by Texas State University (2007), namely:

- Historic and future (see below) ground water elevation data should be consolidated within an electronic database and coordinated with the operation of an appropriate national or state-related database, and
- Given the connection between periodically high water tables and flooding of the Fort, the NHS should renovate at least a select few of the PVC-lined, hand augured and well-point driven piezometers installed by Woods *et al.* (2002) (Figure 25) and renew efforts to monitor ground water elevations.

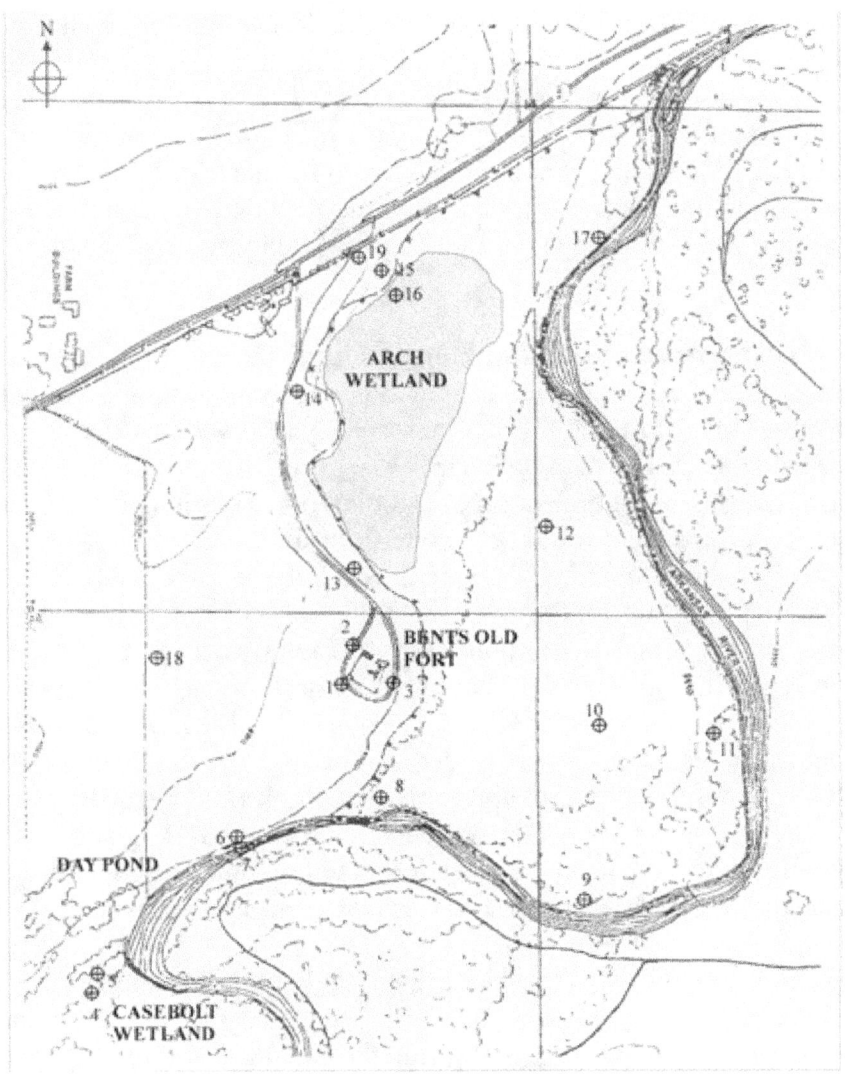

Figure 25. Locations of ground water monitoring wells (1-4,6; 8-15; 18-19) and wetland staff gages (5 and 16) and Arkansas River staff gages (7 and 17) from the study by Woods *et al.* (2002).

With regard to the first recommendation, we suggest that the NHS submit a technical assistance request to the NPS Water Resources Division for assistance with the database and any integration with national/state databases.

With regard to the second recommendation, we suggest the renovation of wells 1, 2 and 3 because of their close association with the Fort and lack of correlation with river stage (see Woods *et al.* 2002) and wells 8 and 11 due to their floodplain location and relatively strong correlation with Arkansas River stage (Figure 25) (see Woods *et al.*). Water table elevations in these wells should be monitored monthly and linked with monthly-monitored levels at the Arkansas River staff gages (sites 7 and 17 in Figure 25) and other appropriate benchmarks (see Woods *et al.* 2002). This will link river stage levels with hydraulic head.

For the present, we do not agree with Woods *et al.* (2002) that a more detailed term study of different water sources and aquifer properties is needed to parse out of the relative effects of

60

river, canal and excess irrigation on water table levels and basement flooding at the fort. Such knowledge, while of heuristic value, would do little in terms of improving of knowledge and mitigating the flooding problem. That basement flooding of the Fort is caused by a combination of high river stage and canal seepage/excess irrigation is of high scientific probability based on the study by Woods *et al*. (2002). Therefore, barring the improbable -- moving the location of the Fort, the NHS should center its energy on mitigation and remediation of the Fort basement, although the available methods are limited. In addition, the NHS should work with such local entities as the Southeast Colorado Resource Conservation and Development Council to understand (hence the need for a renewed effort to monitor ground water levels) and mitigate the amount of excess irrigation and canal leakage flowing towards the NHS. In the future, a study similar to the one proposed by Woods *et al*. may become necessary; if so, the NHS should request technical assistance from NPS Water Resources Division in the development of the project.

Wetland and Riparian Protection

The Arch wetland has increased in size from a saltgrass meadow in the 1980s to a 57-acre wetland in the 1990s apparently in response to the local rise in water table elevation. Woods *et al*. (2002) determined that the primary water source for this wetland is ground water from adjacent uplands. This means that decreasing flow in the Fort Lyon Canal could cause a decrease in the size of the Arch wetland. Similarly, an increase in ground water withdrawals up gradient from the wetland could reduce ground water inflows and reduce the size of the wetland.

The NHS is seeking advice with regard to protection and use of its artificial wetlands, namely, the Day Pond, Day Wetland, and the SW and SE Stock Tanks. Under *Procedural Manual #77-1* (NPS 2008; see page 10), man-made tanks and ponds are considered artificial wetlands. Previously, Noon *et al*. (2005) advised against the suggestion by the County Health Department that the stock tank wetlands be filled to eliminate mosquito breeding and the spread of West Nile virus, unless there were compelling reasons. However, the reasons were not compelling since these artificial wetlands may replace wetland functions that historically occurred along the Arkansas River floodplain, but may have been filled in for agricultural development; filling them would produce a net loss of wetlands and there would be significant costs for environmental compliance and any earthmoving/re-vegetation operations. Any filling of the stock tank wetlands or the Day Pond and Day Wetland, would also have an adverse impact on those wetlands and would require full NEPA compliance (i.e., an environmental assessment or environmental impact statement) and, in most cases, preparation of a wetland statement of findings (SOF). The SOF, attached to the environmental compliance document, documents compliance with NPS wetland policies and procedures (see page 10).

The maintenance of healthy riparian systems is essential in obtaining and sustaining biologically diverse ecosystems. Healthy riparian systems are geologically stable, with stream flow and sediment discharges in dynamic equilibrium with their upland watersheds. The systems' wetland and riparian vegetation has appropriate structural, age, and species diversity. When these attributes are maintained, riparian systems provide forage and cover for wildlife and improve water quality by filtering sediment and recycling nutrients. If, however, any of the essential attributes are missing or degraded, or if the system becomes geologically unstable, widespread erosion many occur that will degrade water quality and cause damage or loss of wetland and riparian habitats.

Texas State University (2007) recommended that bank stabilization could be better understood and quantified by stream and riparian assessments of habitat condition. A riparian assessment tool, *The Process for Assessing Proper Functioning Condition* (Pritchard *et al.* 1998), has been used in the western U.S. to evaluate riparian systems by the U.S. Bureau of Land Management. This technique uses an interdisciplinary team to assess riparian area "functionality" according to 17 hydrologic, vegetation, and stream geomorphologic factors such as erosion, deposition, and channel geometry. It provides an initial screening that can separate areas that are functioning well from those in need of more intensive evaluation or management actions.

Evaluation of the functioning condition is not simply an assessment of the ecological status or serial stage of the vegetation community. Rather, evaluation is based upon the concept that the basic elements of physical habitat must first be in place and functioning properly before management of such things as potential natural vegetation communities can occur.

The basic goal of this process is to classify streams as "proper functioning", "functional at-risk", or "nonfunctional." To do this, the interdisciplinary team evaluates existing literature and conducts field examinations to obtain information that includes the following:

- Identification and description of relic areas;
- Review of historical photos, survey notes, and other documents that indicate historic condition;
- Review of floral and faunal lists;
- Determination of species habitat needs related to species that are or were present;
- Estimation of the frequency and duration of flooding on floodplain and terraces;
- Identification of current vegetation and determination of historical occurrence in the area;
- Determination of entire watershed's general condition and identification of its major landforms; and,
- Identification of limiting factors, both human-induced and natural, and determination of needed remedial actions.

Recommendations
Because the NHS expressed concern about the quality of its wetlands, Texas State University (2007) suggested periodic monitoring of aquatic plants and animals similar to the approach by Gionfriddo *et al.* (2002). We concur with that suggestion and recommend a recurrence interval of every five years. Additionally, we recommend monitoring for a suite of water quality parameters similar to those measured by Woods *et al.* (2002) in the NHS wetlands and would specifically include pH, temperature, dissolved oxygen, specific conductance, nitrogen (dissolved ammonia, total ammonia + organic, dissolved nitrate and nitrite, and dissolved nitrite), and phosphorus (dissolved and ortho-phosphorus dissolved). Sampling locations should be fixed; in the case of the Arch and Casebolt wetlands, sampling should occur at the previous well monitoring sites for those wetlands (see Figure 25). Sampling frequency, initially, should be quarterly, and depending upon the analysis of data for a three to five year timeframe, sampling could occur annually (summer). Additionally, we recommend the establishment of a monitoring

station on the Arch Wetland that is down gradient from the septic system at the Fort – this site should be monitored at least quarterly for nitrogen and phosphorus constituents (see discussion under *Sewage Treatment and Septic Systems* below).

We agree with Texas State University (2007) in recommending the renovation of the monitoring wells established in the Arch and Casebolt wetlands by Woods *et al.* (2002) (wells number 16 and 5, respectively in Figure 25). Ground water elevations should be recorded on a monthly basis and linked with levels at the Arkansas River staff gages (sites 7 and 17 in Figure 25), other ground water monitoring wells, and other appropriate benchmarks (see Woods *et al.* 2002) so that that all sites can be associated with hydraulic head and stream stage (see discussion under *High Water Table and Impacts to Bent's Old Fort*).

We recommend that the artificial wetlands (Day Pond, Day Wetland, and stock tank wetlands) be managed for their wetland functions, which include floodwater storage/attenuation, ground water recharge, amphibian breeding habitat, and other wildlife habitat.

It is recommended that the NHS submit a technical assistance request to the NPS Water Resources Division for an assessment of the riparian conditions along the Arkansas River using *The Process for Assessing Proper Functioning Condition* (Pritchard *et al.* 1998). It is also recommended that the recurrence interval for additional assessments be every five years.

Additionally, the NHS should establish GPS-based photograph points on the banks of the Arkansas River. Photographic monitoring (digitally based) is a simple and inexpensive method to assess changes in stream geomorphology (especially changes since tamarisk removal), the riparian zone, and other physical habitat features that may be associated with site and watershed conditions. A series of photographs would also allow detection of slow, progressive changes in physical habitat features that otherwise might go undetected until the accumulation of impacts is noticeable.

Initially, three photo points should be established: 1) west boundary of NHS looking down river; 2) east boundary of NHS looking up river; and 3) at a point approximately 1.1 miles from either boundary (midpoint of river miles in NHS) and looking both up and down river. Photographs should be taken during the following times each year: 1) baseflow conditions (Figure 13, December-February; 2) ascending limb of hydrograph (Figure 13, May-June); and 3) descending limb of hydrograph (Figure 13, July-September).

Flooding and Stormwater Drainage

Storm drainage around the NHS employee entrance road to the maintenance yard and administration building is a problem during most heavy rain events (Figure 26). A drainage ditch runs along the west side of the road. The ditch has culverts under two access roads to the maintenance yard and one to the administration building. The ditch catches runoff from the surrounding area west of the entry road.

Storm water collects in the ditch at the top (north) end next to the maintenance building and extends south below the cattle guard crossing for the administration building (total length of approximately 300 ft). The ditch essentially acts as a 300-foot-long, linear retention basin with

Figure 26. View of the park employee entrance gate as it passes along the maintenance and administration buildings. The flooding ditch is parallel to the road and between the road and buildings.

no defined outfall. When the ditch is full, excess water likely overflows the high point further south along the edge of the road and continues south toward the river. However, there is no clear channel to indicate where the overflow goes.

Recommendations

One possible solution to the drainage problem is to design an outfall at the south end of the ditch. A ditch and/or culvert extension should be placed to allow positive drainage from the south end of the existing ditch to an area that is lower in elevation. It appears from field observations that one option is to run a culvert to the southeast under the entry road that would day light at a lower elevation in the open field. Since the area seems relatively flat, the culvert may have to be quite long in order to meet grade at a lower elevation in the field. The low areas in the field have water lines and sewer pump station pipes that may or may not allow deposition of sheet flow from the ditch. Another option is to continue the ditch and culverts to the south along the entry road. However, this would end up contributing to the existing drainage system that is further south, which serves the parking lot for the visitor center, and the additional flow may overload that system. The following tasks need to be completed in order to identify, select, and implement the best solution:

- o Complete a detailed topographic survey (no more than one-foot contour elevations) of the entire drainage ditch including culvert inverts, and the survey should also include the area at least 100 feet on either side of the existing ditch, the area around the southern end of the ditch including the road south to the visitor center parking lot, and the open field area (for several hundred feet east of the entry road). Also the water lines, pump station, and sewer pipes that run through the field on the east side of the entry road should be surveyed.

- o Analyze the topography to determine the best solution. Consider the length of culvert necessary depending on the amount of drop in elevation needed to move the water, clogging and maintenance problems, potential erosion problems, and impacts to other infrastructure. Also consider other options including detention basin(s).

64

o Replace all of the culverts in, and dredge, the existing ditch. Since the culvert is acting like a detention basin, the sediment laden water collects in the ditch, slows down, and deposits sediment such that the culverts are half-buried and the ditch is filling with silt.

Sewage Treatment and Septic Systems

There are two septic systems at the NHS: 1) a 1,000-gallon septic tank located west of the visitor parking lot, circa 2000; and 2) a 5,000-gallon septic tank located just west of the fort corral, circa 1970s. The NHS has these septic tanks pumped every three to five years. The smaller, younger septic tank is located on the upper terrace level, outside of the 500-year floodplain, and not adjacent to any water resources. As long as this septic tank is properly maintained we do not expect any leaching of nutrients into down slope water resources, such as the Arch Wetland. However, the larger, older tank is located within the 500-year floodplain and adjacent to wetland and riparian resources. Given the age of this septic tank and its proximity to water resources, nutrients (primarily nitrogen and phosphorus) may become a water quality problem for the Arch Wetland.

Recommendations

We recommend the monitoring of nitrogen and phosphorus as part of a monitoring program for the Arch Wetland (see discussion under the *Wetland and Riparian Protection* issue, above).

Hazardous Waste Management and Spill Contingency Planning

For most of the NPS units like the NHS, internal NPS operations require that hazardous substances, such as petroleum products used in maintenance operations, be stored and handled on a routine basis. Although it is the goal of the NPS to minimize releases of these substances into the environment, accidental releases still occur. The action of those employees who first encounter contamination in the NHS could well determine the severity of the impact(s) on human health and the environment. Therefore, it is important for NPS staff to understand the basic requirements for response to hazardous substance spills.

An even greater concern for hazardous spills in the NHS exists from external operations. The corridors for State Route 194 and the railroad run parallel to the NHS, to the north and south, respectively (see Figure 1). Trucks and trains carry fuel oil, diesel fuel, gasoline, and a variety of agricultural and industrial chemicals along these corridors.

Given these potential pollution pathways, an accidental release of hazardous materials is a continuous threat to the NHS's natural resources. The NPS is severely limited in qualified personnel, spill response equipment, and baseline natural resource information to effectively respond to and evaluate impacts from hazardous spills to the NHS. Emergency response to a major spill requires expertise and field equipment that extends beyond the capabilities of the NPS. In accordance with the National Contingency Plan established under the Clean Water Act, federal agencies are required to have a Spill Contingency Plan (SCP) for emergency response to any spill of oil or hazardous substances for which they are responsible. Furthermore, a Spill Prevention Control and Countermeasure Plan (SPCCP) is required for the NPS to maintain compliance with 40 CFR 112 (EPA Regulations on Oil Pollution Prevention).

At the NHS, petroleum product use is focused around the maintenance yard. There are two above ground petroleum storage tanks in service at the NHS, one for diesel and one for unleaded gasoline. The maintenance facility also stores numerous small containers of paints, hydraulic fluids, motor oil, and gasoline. The NHS has not completed an Oil Spill Prevention and Response Plan.

An environmental compliance audit has completed for the NHS as part of a sevicewide program that requires all NPS facilities to receive an environmental audit. Only one of 11 findings/recommendations is important with regard to water resources – the need for a current hazardous chemical inventory.

The Resource Conservation and Recovery Act (RCRA), as amended by the Hazardous and Solid Waste Act Amendments of 1984 and Title III of the Superfund Amendment Reauthorization Act (SARA Title III) require hazardous waste reduction programs. Executive Order 12873 establishes the goal for federal agencies to reduce their input into the waste stream by 40 percent.

Recommendations

The NHS should strongly consider developing an Oil Spill Prevention and Response Plan. Such a plan would present site-specific information on those locations in the NHS that have the potential to experience such environmental change. In addition, general structural and operational recommendations would be outlined to prevent spills associated with all on-site activities involving the storage and/or use of petroleum products or other hazardous materials. A notification sequence, including emergency contacts, would be provided if a spill occurs. The Plan would be intended for use by all personnel responsible for storage, handling, and removal of hazardous substances at the NHS.

The NHS should implement or improve waste reduction programs through recycling efforts that are applicable to both park staff and visitors.

Water Resources of Bent's Old Fort National Historic Site and Climate Change

Over the past 50 years, Colorado has experienced rising temperatures, increased precipitation, and altered surface water flow due to climate change. The State's eastern plains are experiencing higher temperatures; however, temperature in the Arkansas River Valley has increased by only 0.5° F (U.S. EPA 1997, U.S. Global Change Research Program 2000). Over the next century Colorado is likely to see higher temperatures and more precipitation in some regions while water resources are likely to become less secure (U.S. EPA 1997). Changes in the water cycle will be the vehicle for many impacts of climate change (www.colorado.edu/CO_Climate_Report/index.html).

The Intergovernmental Panel on Climate Change (2007) determined that seasonal temperature changes and overall increased precipitation (Regonda *et al.* 2005), less of which is falling as snow, have led to less snow pack and earlier spring thaw on average in the Rocky Mountains. Between 1978 and 2004, the spring runoff has shifted earlier by two weeks (www.colorado.edu/CO_Climate_Report/index.html). In the future, winter precipitation could increase by 20 to 70 percent, with high altitudes receiving the largest amount (U.S. EPA 1997). This could alter the seasonal flow patterns of major rivers that originate in the Rocky Mountains, intensifying summer droughts in downstream areas as late-summer flows become reduced (IPCC 2007). The change in weather patterns caused by warmer temperatures is expected to increase the risk of drought.

Given observed trends in regional warming and declining snowpack conditions, studies have been conducted to relate potential future climate scenarios to runoff and water resource management impacts. Elgaali *et al.* (2007) and Ojima *et al.* (1999) reported potential climate change impacts on water resources and demands in the Great Plains. Changes in agricultural water demands were evaluated based on climate change scenarios using crop consumptive use methods. Both studies project future increases in crop water consumptive use ranging from 20 to 60 percent by the end of the 21st century.

Based on recent scenario studies, it appears that warming without precipitation change would trigger a seasonal shift toward increased runoff during the winter and decreased runoff during the summer. On the other hand, it also is plausible (based on climate projections) that precipitation increase could occur with regional warming and offset a significant portion of summer runoff decreases associated with warming alone. Garbrecht *et al.* (2004) suggested that the fall through spring months would be most impacted by either a wetter or drier Great Plains climate with stream flow experiencing the greatest impact.

Reduced mountain snowpack, earlier snowmelt, and reductions in spring and summer stream flow volumes originating from snowmelt likely would affect surface water supplies and could trigger heavier reliance on ground water resources (Ryan *et al.* 2008). Also, if a larger percentage of annual precipitation is in the form of intense rain events with high runoff, infiltration and aquifer recharge could be reduced. However, warmer wetter winters could increase the amount of water available for ground water recharge.

Whether water quality conditions improve or decline under climate change depends on several variables including water temperature, flow, runoff rate and timing, and the physical characteristics of the watershed. Climate change has the potential to affect all of these variables. Climate change impacts on surface water systems very likely will affect their capacity to remove pollutants and improve water quality; however, the timing, magnitude, and consequences of these impacts are not well understood (Lettenmaier *et al.* 2008).

Covich *et al.* (1997) predicted Great Plains region impacts on aquatic ecosystems based on two climate change scenarios. Predicted aquatic ecosystem impacts were based primarily on changes in water temperatures, nutrients, and food sources. For example, increased summer air temperatures could increase dry season aquatic temperatures and affect fisheries habitat. The confidence in their predictions for aquatic impacts is higher for the southern Great Plains area, including the NHS.

We recommend that the NHS submit a technical assistance request to the NPS Climate Change Response Program for the application of the Climate Change Scenario Planning process to explore potential futures at the NHS based on the most recent science.

Literature Cited

Bossong, C. 2000. Analysis of hydrologic factors that affect ground-water levels in the Arkansas River alluvial aquifer near La Junta, Colorado 1959-1999. Water Resources Investigation Report 00-4047. U.S. Geological Survey, Denver, CO.

Brix, K. and many others. 2001. Effects of sulfate on the acute toxicity of selenate to freshwater organisms. Environ. Toxicity an and Chemistry 20(5):1037-1045.

Burkhalter, J. and T. Gates. 2005. Agroecological impacts from salinization and waterlogging in an irrigated river valley. ASCE Journal of Irrigation and Drainage Engineering 11(2):197-209.

Colorado Department of Public Health and the Environment. No date. Colorado EMAP— Ecological Monitoring and Assessment Report. Water Quality Control Division, Denver, CO.

Colorado Department of Public Health and the Environment. 2002. Status of water quality in Colorado, 2002. Denver, Colorado.

Colorado Department of Public Health and the Environment. 2006. Status of water quality in Colorado, 2006. Denver, CO.

Colorado Department of Public Health and the Environment 2007. Regulation #32, classifications and numeric standards for the Arkansas River basin. Amended August 13, 2007 and effective December 31, 2007.

Colorado Water Quality Control Division. 2002. Rebuttal statement – matter of revisions to the classifications and numeric standards for the Arkansas River Basin (Regulation #32). June 14, 2002. Denver, CO.

Cowardin, l., V. Carter, F. Golet, and E. LaRoe. 1979. Classification of wetlands and deepwater habitats of the United States. U.S. Fish and Wildlife Service, Office of Biological Services, Washington, D.C.

Covich, A., S. Fritz, P. Lamb, R. Marzolf, W. Matthews, K. Poiani, E. Prepas, M. Richman, T. Winter. 1997. Potential effects of climate change on aquatic ecosystems of the Great Plains of North America. Hydrological Processes 11(8):993–1021.

DeCamps, H. 1993. River margins and environmental change. J. Ecol. Appl. 3:441-445.

Donnelly, P. and T. Gates. 2005. Assessing irrigation-induced selenium and iron in the lower Arkansas River Valley in Colorado. Proceedings of ASCE EWRI.

Elgaali, E., L. Garcia and D. Ojima. 2007. High resolution modeling of the regional impacts of climate change on irrigation water demand. Climatic Change 84:3–4.

Fenneman, N. and D. Johnson. 1946. Physical divisions of the United States. U.S. Geological Survey, scale 1:7,000,000.

Garbrecht, J, M. Van Liew, and G. Brown. 2004. Trends in precipitation, streamflow, and evapotranspiration in the Great Plains of the United States. Journal of Hydrologic Engineering 9(5):360–367.

Gardner, M. 2004. Bent's Fort on the Arkansas: Bent's Old Fort NHS Historic Resource Study.Unpublished Report. Prepared for National Park Service, Contract #P1310990308.

Gates, T. and M. Grismer. 1989. Irrigation and drainage strategies in salinity-affected regions. J. Irrigation and Drainage Engineering 115(2): 255-284.

Gates, T., L. Garcia, and J. Labadie. 2006. Toward optimal water management in Colorado's Lower Arkansas River Valley: monitoring and modeling to enhance agriculture and environment. Colorado Water Resources Research Institute Completion Report No. 205, Colorado State University, Fort Collins, CO.

Gates, T. and many others. 2009. Assessing selenium contamination in irrigated stream-aquifer system of Arkansas River, Colorado. J. Environ. Qual. 38:2344-2356.

Gionfriddo, J., D. Culver, and J. Stevens. 2002. Biological survey of Bent's Old Fort National Historic Site, Otero County, Colorado. Unpublished Report to National Park Service by Colorado Natural Heritage Program, La Junta, CO.

Gionfriddo, J. and J. Stevens. 2003. Survey of Bent's Old Fort National Historic Site for breeding birds and anurans, May 2002. Unpublished Report to National Park Service by Colorado Natural Heritage Program, La Junta, CO.

Goff, K., M. Lewis, M. Person and L. Konikow. 1998. Simulated effects of irrigation on salinity in the Arkansas River valley in Colorado. Groundwater 36(1):76-86.

Hughes, J. 2010. Trip report to Superintendent, Bent's Old Fort National Historic Site, for travel to the NHS on June 24, 1010. National Park Service, Water Resources Division, Fort Collins, CO.

Intergovernmental Panel on Climate Change. 2007. Regional climate projections, section 11.5: North America. Chapter 11 *in* Working Group I: the physical science basis of climate change. Cambridge University Press, London.

Lettenmaier, D., D. Major, L. Poff, and S. Running. 2008. "Water Resources."The Effects of Climate Change on Agriculture, Land Resources, WaterResources, and Biodiversity in the United States. A report by theU.S. Climate Change Science Program and the subcommittee on GlobalChange Research. Washington, D.C.

Lewis, M. 1998. Relations of main-stem reservoir operations and specific conductance in the lower Arkansas River, Southeastern Colorado. USGS Fact Sheet 166-97. US Geological Survey, Pueblo, CO.

Maier, K., C. Foe, R. Ogle, M.Williams, A. Knight, P. Kiffney, and L. Melton. 1987. The dynamics of selenium in aquatic ecosystems. Trace substances in environmental health. University of Missouri.

Mueller, D., L. DeWeese, A. Garner and T. Spruill. 1991. Reconnaissance investigation of water quality, bottom sediment, and biota associated with irrigation drainage in the middle Arkansas River Basin, Colorado and Kansas, 1988-1989. U.S. Geological Survey Water Resources Investigations Report 91-4060. Denver, CO.

MWH. 2005. Draft Water Resources Technical Report for the Southern Delivery System Environmental Impact Statement. Prepared for Bureau of Reclamation, Eastern Colorado Area Office, Loveland, CO.

MWH. 2008. Water Quality Technical Report for the Southern Delivery System Environmental Impact Statement. Prepared for U.S. Bureau of Reclamation, Eastern Colorado Area Office, Loveland, CO.

Nadler, C. and S. Schumm. 1981. Metamorphosis of South Platte and Arkansas Rivers, eastern Colorado. Physical Geography 1981(2):95-115.

Naiman, R., H. DeCamps and M. Pollock. 1993. The role of riparian corridors in maintaining regional biodiversity. Ecol. Appl. 3:209-212.

Naiman, R. and H. DeCamps. 1997. The ecology of interfaces: riparian zones. Ann. Rev. Ecol. Syst. 28:621-658.

National Park Service. 1994. Draft environmental impact statement and general management plan, development concept plan. Bent's Old Fort National Historic Site. La Junta, CO.

National Park Service. 1998. Baseline water quality inventory and analysis, Bent's Old Fort National Historic Site. Tech. Rept. NPS/NRWRD/NRTR—98/165. Water Resources Division, Fort Collins, CO.

National Park Service. 2003. Clean Water Act water quality designated uses and impairments for Bent's Old Fort National Historic Site. Tech. Report NPS/NRWRD/NRTR-2003/302, Water Resources Division, Fort Collins, CO.

National Park Service. 2005. Geologic Resources Evaluation Report, Bent's Old Fort National Historic Site. NPS D-74, Geologic Resources Division, Denver, CO.

National Park Service. 2006. Management Policies. U.S. Department of Interior. Washington, D.C.

National Park Service. 2008. National Park Service Procedural Manual #77-1: Wetland Protection.

Natural Resources Conservation Service. 2007. Rapid assessment for Lake Meredith watershed, hydrologic unit code 110200005. Lakewood, CO.

Nestler, T. and many others. 1999. Inventory and status of Arkansas River native fishes in Colorado. Colorado Division of Wildlife, Denver, CO.

Noon, K., M. Martin, and J. Wagner. 2005. Report for travel to Bent's Old Fort National Historic Site, October 20-21, 2004. Bent's Old Fort National Historic Site, La Junta, CO.

Ojima D., L. Garcia, E. Elgaali, K. Miller, T. Kittel, and J. Lackett. 1999. Potential climate change impacts on water resources in the Great Plains."Journal of the American Water Resources Association 35(6):1443–1454.

Ortiz, R., M. Lewis, and M. Radell. 1998. Water quality assessment of the Arkansas River Basin, Southeastern, Colorado, 1990-1993. USGS Water Resources Investigations Report 97-411. Denver, CO.

Paul, M, J. Gerritsen, C. Hawkins, and E. Leppo. 2005. Development of biological assessment tools for Colorado. Prepared for Colorado Department of Public Health and the Environment. Tetra Tech Inc., Owing Mills, MD.

Perkins, D., H. Sosinski, K. Cherwin, and T. Zettner. 2005a. Southern Plains Network vital signs monitoring plan: phase I. National Park Service, Southern Plains Network, Johnson City, TX.

Perkins, D., H. Sosinski, K. Cherwin, and T. Zettner. 2005b. Southern Plains Network vital signs monitoring plan: phase I appendices. National Park Service, Southern Plains Network, Johnson City, TX.

Pritchard, D. and many others. 1998. Riparian area management – a user guide to assessing proper functioning condition and the supporting science for lotic areas. U.S. Bureau of Land Management, Tech. Rept. 1737-15, Denver, CO.

Radosevich, G.E., K.C. Nobe, D. Allardice, and C. Kirkwood. 1976. Evolution and Administration of Colorado Water Law: 1876-1976. Water Resource Publications, Fort Collins CO.

Regonda, S.K., B. Rajagopalan, M. Clark, and J. Pitlick. 2005. "Seasonal cycle shifts in hydroclimatology over the western United States." Journal of Climate 18(2): 372–384.

Rosgen, D. 1996, Applied River Morphology. Wildland Hydrology Books, Pagosa Springs, Co.

Ryan, M., S. Archer, R. Birdsey, C. Dahm, L. Heath, J. Hicke, D. Hollinger, T. Huxman, G. Okin, R. Oren, J. Randerson, and W. Schlesinger. 2008. Land Resources. The Effects of climate change on agriculture, land resources, water resources, and biodiversity in the United States. Report by the U.S. Climate Change Science Program and the subcommittee on Global Change Research. Washington, D.C.

Sares, Matthew A. and Vincent Matthews. "Ground Water Atlas of Colorado." Colorado Geological Survey. 23 Nov 2007 <http://geosurvey.state.co.us/wateratlas/index.asp>.

Schumm, S. 1969. River metamorphosis. J. Hydraulics Division, American Society of Civil Engineers Proceedings, 95:255-273.

Seiler, R., J. Skorupa, and L. Peltz. 1999. Areas susceptible to irrigation-induced selenium contamination of water and biota in the western United States. U. S. Geological Survey Circular 1180, Denver, CO.

State of Colorado. 2008. Guide to Colorado well permits, water Rights, and water administration, January, 2008. Department of Natural Resources, Division of Water Resources, Denver, CO.

Stevens, J., K. Forrest, S. Neid, and M. Fink. 2007. Bent's Old Fort National Historic Site: Vegetation Classification and Mapping. Natural Resource Technical Report NPS/SOPN/NRTR—2007/049. National Park Service, Fort Collins, Colorado.

Swenson, F. 1970. Meandering of the Arkansas River since 1833 near Bent's Old Fort, Colorado. U.S. Geological Survey Professional Paper 700-B, Denver, CO.

Tetra Tech. 2007. Draft Lower Arkansas Watershed Plan. Prepared for Southeast Colorado Resource Conservation and Development, Lamar, CO.

Texas State University. 2007. Review of and recommendations for hydrologic-monitoring activities in southern plains network, National Park Service. Edwards Aquifer Research and Data Center, San Marcos, TX.

Tisdale-Hein, Rinda E. 2006. Survey of fish and plant species in Arch Wetland and Arkansas River at Bent's Old National Historic Site. Unpublished Report. Bent's Old Fort National Historic Site, La Junta, CO.

U.S. Army Corps of Engineers. 1986. Phase I, General Design Memorandum. Unpublished Report, Bent's Old Fort National Historic Site, La Junta, CO.

U.S. Environment Protection Agency. 1998. Report on peer consultation workshop and selenium aquatic toxicity and bioaccumulation. EPA-822-R-98-007.

U.S. Environmental Protection Agency. 1997. Climate change and Colorado. Climate and Policy Assessment Division, www.epa.gov/globalwarmingimpacts.

U.S. Geological Survey. 2002. Changes in ground-water levels in selected wells in the Arkansas River alluvial aquifer downstream from Pueblo Reservoir, Southeastern Colorado, 1965-2001. U.S. Geological Survey Fact Sheet 023-02. Pueblo, CO.

U.S. Global Change Research Program. 2000. Climate change impacts on the United States: the potential consequences of climate variability and change. Chapter 8 *in* J. Smith, R Richels, and B. Miller, eds., Potential consequences of climate variability and change for the western United States, Washington, D.C.

Wallner. 2006. Long-range Interpretive Plan. Bent's Old Fort National Historic Site. La Junta, CO.

Ward, J., 1998. Riverine landscapes: biodiversity patterns, disturbance regimes, and aquatic conservation. Biol. Cons. 83:269–278.

Watts, K. and J. Lindner-Lunsford. 1992. Evaluation of proposed water management alternatives to lower the high water table in the Arkansas River Valley near La Junta, Colorado. Water Resources Investigation Report 91-4046. U.S. Geological Survey, Denver, CO.

Weist, W., E. Jenkins, and A. Horr. 1965. Geology and occurrence of ground water in Otero County and southern part of Crowley County, Colorado. U.S. Geological Survey Water-Supply Paper 1799.

Woods, S., L. MacDonald, and D. Campbell. 2002. The cause of basement flooding at Bents Old Fort National Historic Site, Colorado. Unpublished Report, Bent's Old Fort National Historic Site, La Junta, CO.

Zielinski, R., S. Asher-Bolinder and A. Meier. 1995. Uraniferous waters of the Arkansas River valley, Colorado, U.S.A.: a function of geology and land use. Applied Geochemistry 10(2):133-144.

NPS 417/105853, October 2010